Life is Good Today

*Freshly Brewed Devotions for
Your Coffee and Sanity Breaks*

DR. THOMAS E ENGEL

Copyright © 2016 Thomas E Engel.

All rights reserved. No part of this book may be reproduced, stored, or transmitted by any means—whether auditory, graphic, mechanical, or electronic—without written permission of both publisher and author, except in the case of brief excerpts used in critical articles and reviews. Unauthorized reproduction of any part of this work is illegal and is punishable by law.

ISBN: 978-1-4834-4240-2 (sc)
ISBN: 978-1-4834-4239-6 (e)

Because of the dynamic nature of the Internet, any web addresses or links contained in this book may have changed since publication and may no longer be valid. The views expressed in this work are solely those of the author and do not necessarily reflect the views of the publisher, and the publisher hereby disclaims any responsibility for them.

Any people depicted in stock imagery provided by Thinkstock are models, and such images are being used for illustrative purposes only. Certain stock imagery © Thinkstock.

Lulu Publishing Services rev. date: 01/04/2015

Dedication

To my son, Clayton, who is everything about God's love and strength. Thanks for your courage in the "tough" times.

At Counters of Diners

I am one of those guys who can't remember another guy's name two minutes after I am introduced to him, but I can remember a story. Any story that someone tells me locks into my brain, and it stays there for long periods of time. I am curious about the world and love adventure. When I read or hear a story, I put myself into the action and feel all the parts of the story.

While growing up my mom managed this muffin shop that was on the square in town. It opened at six, and she had to get up at four to get there by five to start the ovens up and start baking.

After school, I would ride my bike and get a blueberry muffin that didn't sell in the morning and wash it down with a big glass of milk, and I always felt like a big deal because everybody knew me as Lorraine's kid. Everyone in town really liked my mom, and I kind of got the royal treatment.

The shop had this counter where a lot the guys in town stopped by to have a muffin and coffee and talk about politics and the Cubs. My dad said that men just need to get their elbows on something like a counter or a bar and talk a lot about nothing.

I listened to the guys and really got into their stories, and when I went away to college, I found that it was in me to hang out in diners and get all the scoops on whatever were the latest stories from the messes in government to how the upper managements of ball clubs never really know how to put a winning team together.

In college, one of the first things that I did was to find a good diner to hang out in. I found this place called the Parkmoor. The restaurant is known for its crisp bacon, perfect sunny side up eggs, and near plate-size hamburgers. It was my routine to spend Tuesday and Thursday nights from ten to midnight there drinking cups of coffee, heavily diluted with cream. My favorite booth was in the back where I could see the front door by a reflection in a large mirror on the wall.

When I needed a break from studying, I would watch the mirror and observe the people coming and going. It was like a parade of different floats, each person having a different theme. The factory workers coming off of second shift would drink cups of coffee while sharing their stories of hard-nosed supervisors. Nurses would come and get loaded up on nicotine-smoking cigarettes before their shift at the hospital. And red-eyed truckers who were crossing the country would eat and give their minds a rest from the hypnotic trance of the road.

It was three weeks before Christmas, and I was spending more time at the Parkmoor cramming for finals. The waitresses were kind to me. At that time of night, the place would not fill up, and they liked someone sitting at their table. I would leave them the best tip that a college student could afford.

This night I did not spend much time looking in the mirror. I had a long physics exam the next day. The waitress came and heated up my milky coffee. I would not have noticed her, but except that she was singing "Silent Night" along with Glen Campbell that was on the sound system. She had a good and clear voice.

I stopped my studying to hear her sing. As she moved from table to table, I noticed that the other customers stopped their talking to listen to her. When she got to the nurses and shift workers, they started to sing with her. The trucker on his cell phone told his dispatcher that he would call him back, and he started to sing. The waitress kept making her rounds with her coffee pot, filling cups and inspiring others with her lovely voice. I even started singing. And that one time performance of the "Parkmoor Choir" slapped a good feeling in my heart. I think that if God came to a smelly stable of cow dung, then he could come to a smoky greasy restaurant near a college campus in St. Louis.

I kept going there and saw the staff turnover a few times, I knew a few cooks and waitresses from the beginning, and they threw me a little party when I graduated. After college, I got this job that made me travel around quite a bit. It fit me perfect because as a single guy I got to eat at all kinds of diners and flirt with waitresses who called me sweetie, but I knew they called all their customers sweetie or honey, but I liked to take it personal, anyway.

I was on the road after a long appointment, and it was after lunch time, so I stopped at a truck stop. The place was almost empty, but its messy look and the stink of a recent busy lunch lingered. The smoke of hot grease hung in the air. Half-filled coffee mugs and crumpled napkins were scattered on the counter.

I sat down on a stool in the front of the least cluttered spot on the counter. The waitress came over and removed a water glass and wiped off the counter in front of me. She never looked up, but she mumbled that she would be back to take my order.

I didn't mind her curtness. Probably like me, she had endured a long morning that had extended way into the afternoon. My stomach gurgled as the waitress came back, and I ordered a burger and fries.

The waitress still didn't look above her pad, so I decided to take the initiative to be more personal.

"Thanks Gwen," I said, noticing the name on her badge.

She looked at me long enough to say what she had to say, "My name is Sophia. The boss likes for us to wear name tags. I forgot mine, so I put on this one." She left for the kitchen.

I grabbed a part of a newspaper and read the headlines. Nothing in the paper caught my attention. The last few people had paid their checks and went out to battle a wind that was kicking up.

Next to the cash register was a large pickle jar with a young girls' picture on it. A small poster said she suffered from leukemia, and it asked customers to give their change to help pay medical bills. A layer of change and bills covered the bottom of the jar.

When Sophia came with my burger, she asked if I needed a refill on my drink. I told her, "Yes," and pointed to the jar. "It's a shame that a family has to go through a thing like that."

Sophia looked me straight in the eye and said, "That kind of thing happens every day."

I could tell Sophia was trying to send me a message, buy I didn't get it. I left it alone to finish my burger and to get out to fight the wind, too, and finish the day. I went to the cash register to pay my bill, and I dumped my change into the pickle jar.

As I was going back to leave my tip, I caught the other side of the pickle jar. A small note on it said, "Sophia's child."

I stopped and looked at Sophia. "I'm so sorry. It must be hard."

She looked at me, and her expression changed. "Today was just a bad day. It'll get better."

I couldn't think of anything to say at the moment. What can a stranger say to another about a sad personal part of a life? I told her that I would pray for her. Sophia said, "That's all that we can do. It's the best we can do."

I nodded and left. My stomach was full, but I couldn't have felt emptier. I never made it back to that truck stop and wonder whenever I am in a diner like that one what had happened to Sophia and her kid.

I kept that job for a few years, but then I got married and had my son, so I got another job that kept me closer to home. I didn't eat out as much, but on my way to the train I got use to going to this coffee shop by the station in the morning to read the paper and listen to the latest chat on current events. What I discovered was that I started to get real picky about my coffee. Things changed of my taste for coffee. I liked the rich dark strong coffee that the shop offered.

Walking into the shop for the first time, I smiled the aroma of good coffee. I tried different kinds of coffee, and I settled on Sumatra. It wasn't long before I would walk up to counter and Kelly, the manager, would have my coffee for me.

There weren't any counters in the shop, only small table and chairs with a fireplace with combatable stuffed chairs. In the corner of the shop was a small couch where I glanced through the headlines and checked my emails. A group of retired guys were there in the early mornings, and I got to know them a little through casual conversation. Fred was a teacher who came to the shop to write his memories about his teaching career. He said he has been working on it for about five years and is on chapter sixty-two and had a ways to go before he thought it was finished.

Burt just retired and is trying to find what he should be doing and is restless and is already talking about getting a part-time consultant thing going. George has been retired for several years and walks two miles before he comes to get coffee and reads the obituaries to see if anybody he knows has died. Then, there is Joe who is the youngest guy at fifty-four and is on disability after hurting his back at work, and would say that every day was a great day in the Lord when he saw you and, even though he lost a son in the Gulf War.

I am at the coffee shop now finishing this essay up. I like the energy here, like back when I was a kid and in college and finding out who I am through the people I meet. Here, I feel connected with other people and I get the feeling I belong to something bigger than myself. It's were I reflect on God's creation and his will for me in all that is happening around me.

Life is about people and places and how I am involved in all of that. So I sit at tables in the corners of diners, put my elbows on counters, or sit on a couch and drink coffee and take bites out of a raisin scone and watch the world go by in all of its sorrows and joys. This is how I wrote most of the devotions in this book. Drinking coffee and contemplating God's Word has been an awesome combination for my soul.

Life is Good Today

In college, my first year English professor, Mrs. Wagner, began each class period with an inspiring saying on the board. She had us journal on each saying. I remember one that still often pops up in my mind, "Each day create a new you again, again, and again."

It was the repeating of the word "again" that made me do some thinking back then and quite a bit now. One "new" me a day seems enough, and it would seem to take a lot of work to keep creating a new person throughout a whole day. I am not sure what I wrote back then. Back then in college, I thought I had it all together, so probably nothing too deep, but since then life has dealt out some hard challenges, and through the years, I have gotten to feeling pretty worn, and that repeated word "again" keeps saying something to me.

The freezer breaks down and all the meat has gone bad, a copier jams just when there is a deadline to meet, and news from the doctor about a lump that needs to be treated immediately-it's this kind of stuff that can all happen in a short period of time and be overwhelming.

Things have a way of piling up, but it's in these times that we have the opportunity to learn something about ourselves. Something that I did not get when I was young but am getting more now, and that is that life's best lessons come from failure. I did not like to fail when I was young. Things going wrong messed with my ego, but now I am learning that during difficult times, we can search for what is really in us.

God gives me opportunities throughout every day for me to make me what I want me to be. To be sure, we are not in control of the situations that come our way. When driving down the road, I can't do anything about getting a flat tire, but I can choose the way I react when I hear the thuds of a tire going flat. This is a moment when I can create a new me. I can react with impatience and anxiousness that will cause just more stress and more problems because I am out of a good mindset, or I can accept the situation for what it is, change the flat tire, and thank God that I am safe and back on the road.

The only way to learn about patience is to be in an anxious time. We learn about courage by experiencing fear. When we are feeling weak, and it does not seem we can go on, we can find strength and perseverance. In the times of discouragement, we can see that there is hope.

The important word here is the word "can." God makes available to us all that we need, so it is possible that we can have in every situation things like patience, courage, strength, perseverance, and hope. God is good and is always giving us good things.

Jesus is the ultimate teacher. He is the best authority on the kingdom of God because he is the kingdom of God, and he knows where people are at and meets them in their situations. It is not that the heaven is so hard to understand, but we have a tendency to be stubborn and have hard natures and do not let the simple truths of God's love and will for us into our minds and hearts.

Jesus wanted people to know about God's kingdom, and he knew that they only way to get through to people was to show them the kingdom, so that is why Jesus went to the blind, deaf, lame, and sick, and performed miracles, even raised the dead. He taught people in parables, and he shared simple stories that met people where they were at and that they could relate to.

Jesus was trying to get people to understand that the kingdom of God was about new life in him. In Christ we have always have the opportunity to come to him with our problems and the burden of the guilt and shame of sin, and find strength and forgiveness.

By the grace of God, there is never a "bad" day. I want to be careful not to minimalize our problems. There is no doubt that bad things do happen to us. Peter tried to walk on water with Jesus, but lacked faith and began to sink; he boldly says he will die with Jesus, but then later he denies his friend and Lord. That was a truly "bad" day for him as he wept. Not getting it right was a pattern with Peter at first; he had a lot to learn and kept having to start over again.

I think Mrs. Wagner was trying to get over inflated college students to be open to new ideas. God is asking, "What are you making for this day?" I want to say on any day, "Life is good today." As things might happen in a day that want to discourage me, it does not mean that this day has to be bad. I can say when anything happens, "Life is good today."

When I go to visit my great niece, I like to buy her a little gift like new crayons or a book. The last time I went for a visit I bought her play dough. I had forgotten how much fun it is to mold and shape something with your hands. With her imagination and little fingers she made a dog. She said, "Look, Uncle Tom, my new little puppy." I said, "Yes, I can see it." I really just saw a ball of play dough with some thumb impressions in it. The great thing about play dough is that is can be kept being made into something new. "You can have it if you want," she said. It's on my desk with a little note, "Life is good today."

How to Repurpose Your Life

While I was channel surfing, I landed on a show that has become one of my favorites. It is about these two men who travel around the country picking through other people's stuff. They ask collectors for permission to hunt for second hand treasures that might be tucked away in their basements, garages, and yards.

When they find something that they think they could fix up and resell, they make an offer. Most of the time people have a difficult time letting go of their dear possessions, and these guys have to make a hard deal. They need to figure out what they have to pay to get the stuff and what it will cost to fix it up, so they can turn some kind of profit.

A lot of times these things are used for other than their original purposes. An old gas station sign will be touched up and be used in a home's recreation room to give it a kind of nostalgic feel. Or maybe an old toy like a little car made of iron could become a paper weight in an executive's office as a conversational piece. The show calls this repurposing.

I've read where aluminum can be recycled over and over again and a can made out of aluminum can be recycled and then be used as part of an airplane or machinery. Aluminum can be recycled and repurposed for many other uses over and over again.

I got to thinking that if old broken stuff can be repurposed and aluminum can be crushed, melted, and made into something with a new purpose, so maybe I, at the age of fifty-five with the beginning signs of arthritis and having many mistakes made in the past, can find new purpose and meaning.

In any life, it is never impossible to start over again, but I have found that repurposing is a process. It takes time to find a new purpose again. After the death of a loved one, a job loss, or a divorce, it will take time to find new meaning in life, but a new purpose can develop.

Jesus stepped onto a beach one day and talked to a few men who were fishing, and he called them to become his disciples. Their lives would constantly be changing as they became students of a master teacher and learned about the kingdom of God to then became witnesses of the greatest event on earth, Jesus' death and resurrection, and finally, they were the ones to get out into the world and start the early church proclaiming that the forgiveness of sins and eternal life is for all who believe.

I can just see many people in the Bible scratching their heads when God told them to begin a new purpose in their lives. Noah was to build an ark in the middle of dry land; Moses was to lead the nation of Israel out of slavery to a promised land with a hard headed Pharaoh, a sea, and a wilderness between them and that land. David, only a young man was to slay a giant and to go from being a shepherd to a king, and God had Paul go from being a persecutor of Christians to become a great apostle. It all shows we never know what new purposes God will have for a life.

Jesus came to repurpose everyone and everything, even love. One day, he sits with his disciples and gives them a new commandment. This new commandment is really an old commandment made new again. It is, too, repurposed. In Jesus telling his disciples to love, he is saying what God told to Moses in his commandments on Mount Sinai, but to his disciples the commandment to love is new again as Jesus knows what he will do on the cross by taking the punishment for the sins of the world.

Every day we are forgiven of our sins and in that forgiveness we have new life to love again. If we did not have that forgiveness and new life, our love would be coming from guilt and shame and bitterness and old bad habits and hurts and that love would be a sour love. Jesus has come to remove all of what gets in the way of real love and gives us chance to live again in a new way.

Love takes on a new meaning and purpose every day that we are in Christ. We are not to love like we did yesterday and the love we have today will be different tomorrow. Our love is different each day because every day we are strengthened by God with his love for us that is always overflowing.

It is a good exercise to imagine a life of love with every person in every situation, whether it is at home, work, school, or community. Then, when we see how good that can be, we can take the steps to get there. Our overall purpose is to take the steps of admitting where we have gone wrong, seek forgiveness for that wrong, and in that forgiveness, we can approach life with a new purpose.

Every time I get up from a chair, my knees remind me that I am not the same person I was a few years ago. If life is about anything, it is about accepting changes. Life is different now, and that is okay. I have the opportunity to bring in all the bad and good of my life and have it come together for new purposes. I am not always sure of all the specifics of my purpose every day, so I keep going and still do things like jogging with my aching knees knowing Jesus may call me at any moment to move in a new direction with a new purpose.

On Being Young Again

The other day I was walking down the stairs of my apartment on my way to work when my landlord's fifteen year son asked with a bright smile, "Hey Tom, do you mind if I use your deck today. I have a project." I was thinking here is an ambitious young man getting up early in the summer to do work around the place. Yea, probably work that has been directed by his mom and dad, but he still is up and willing with a good attitude. Then he says, "I am making a Frisbee golf course, and your deck is part of the course that I am designing." I gave a little laugh and said, "Sure, no problem. Let me know how it turns out." Getting in my car I thought, "Wow, wouldn't it be great to be young again."

Here I am on my way to a full day of obligations and commitments and now thinking about the freedom of youth. I know I am blessed with work that I enjoy, but it's been awhile since I had a day to play.

At fifty-five, I have trouble saying that I am old. I try to take care of myself by eating right and to keep a daily modest exercise program. Often I jog around a path in an old cemetery. Many people use this path to exercise because it is tranquil with flowers and trees, and it happens that the circular path is about one mile.

No matter how many times that I jog around that cemetery, the fact is that one day I will be planted in it someday. We really don't like to hear the fact that we are not getting any younger. Life changes quickly, and I am not sure even if I notice that rapid changes of technology today. New gadgets are coming out every day. Maps have changed their borders in my life time. The world is changing before our eyes that even a news junkie like me has difficulty keeping up with it.

The winds of change are always blowing over our heads. Most of those changes are in our bodies that are showing more steps to old age and slowing down than to youth and vigor. It's said we are only as old as we feel, and a good attitude does help, but reality says the clock is ticking, and it won't stop.

I like to think I am like pair of jeans. I haven't bought a new pair of jeans for years. One of the pockets is wearing and the bottoms are a frayed of my favorite jeans. I'm not quite ready to buy a new pair yet. My niece thinks my jeans are cool with the holes. Like my jeans, I like to think that I'm getting cooler with age.

Okay, for a minute I can think I am young again, but as the jeans will eventually fall apart thread by thread, so will I. Kind of a depressing thought, isn't it?

In my devotion time, I found a comforting verse from Psalm 37:25, "I have been young, and now I am old, yet I have not seen the righteous forsaken…" What I have been getting from this is that as we look back at our lives, in one way or another, God has always taken care of us. This promise is our hope at all times.

A good formula for having hope in something is that if you can see it, touch it, and smell it, don't put any hope in it. So what do we put our hope in? By definition faith requires that a person trust in something that is out of our human reach.

When we make our own peace and joy, they will never be whole and complete. As we live our lives, our minds are conflicted with stress and anxiousness, our feelings by their very nature go up and down, situations will always be happening, and all thing things wear out.

Our blessing from God is that He has given us the gift of faith. This gift comes from Christ's hands that are scarred from taking the punishment for our sins on the cross and from God's heart of love to our minds, hearts, and spirits. Although we and this earth are wasting away, we are being renewed every day by the Holy Spirit that brings us power from the highest points of heaven.

I like to go with the idea that I can rejoice that I am conflicted at times. The difficult things that come into my life challenge my mind, check that

I do have feelings, and all the aches and pains of my body show that I am alive. Situations will always be coming, and they show that I am an active player in this world. I want to be engaged with others, even if it causes me some heartache at times.

But the grace of God, we have choices. We can choose to go the human route of always trying to fix our messes, or we can live by faith and know all is okay as it is, and go through and not around problems knowing they are bringing us to the greatest blessing of all-to be renewed in all ways to the glory of God.

So in a sense although outwardly I am getting older and all the anti-wrinkle cream in the world can't stop that, I am getting younger by the minute because inwardly I am growing by faith. I boiled it all down to one question that I ask the guy in the mirror every day, even when he looks puffy with age, "What is God bringing new that is young and strong in me today?"

The answer to that question can be an awesome adventure of faith, so I go out in the day with that thought to meet the day.

Crock Pot Wonders

Cruising down the frozen food aisle with my shopping cart that was already halfway loaded with several cereal boxes and a couple gallons of milk, I saw a guy opening and closing the freezer doors. In between opening and closing the doors, he took out boxes of frozen dinners and tossed them in his cart with a monotonous motion without looking at what was in the boxes. I didn't mean to stare at him, but I could not help wondering if I looked this uninspired as I shopped the frozen food aisle.

At the check-out line, I dumped out the cereal boxes and frozen dinners and looked at the magazines and saw a cooking magazine with an article that spoke right to me and my microwave. I skimmed through the first page. It talked about getting out of the frozen food section and discovering the satisfying taste of crock pot wonders. I bought the magazine and read it that week.

The next time that I went to the store I had a grocery list and went to the fresh vegetable section and enjoyed the smells and colors. It was like being out on a farm. The next morning, I got up a little earlier than usual and followed the easy directions for Chicken Fresca with Chardonnay. In a few minutes of slicing vegetables and dashing some spices, I was done.

Coming home that night it was probably what it would be like entering Martha Stewarts' home at dinner time. My apartment never smelled that good. A neighbor took a whiff and asked what restaurant I ordered out from.

The meal was delicious, and it was a wonder as promised. I thought cooking was for other people, but anyone can cook and have good food.

A good meal does not need to be complicated. That evening I started thinking about what other things in my busy life that needed to change. Life can be simple and good. What other things were I missing out on because I was over-crowding myself with things I thought I needed but really didn't need at all?

We tend to make life complicated. I have apps on my phone that I do not even know what they are for. I have buttons on my microwave that I never use. On my car's console there is a small computer that has more programs that anyone should use, especially while driving. Don't get me wrong-I love my laptop, but I found I had to get up earlier every day to check all my emails and messages on the all of the social media that is out there. I found that all I was doing was staring at screens all day.

We have convinced ourselves that we must be multi-taskers. In our attempts to do many things, we have lost our focus to do one thing well. I found myself adding so much to life to try to make it full and meaningful that I lost its true purpose to enjoy simple pleasures, like making a good meal.

This problem is just not a modern day thing. Back in Jesus' times, the Pharisees said there was always more to be done. They kept adding to rules and customs from how to wash one's hands to cleaning pots to worship. And it got to the point that they missed out on some of the more important things in life like helping someone who needed help on the Sabbath, which to them in their interpretation of the Sabbath, it was a day of total rest, so a person could not be healed on that day.

Jesus knew what to do in every circumstance because he kept things simple. He brought everything together under one thought. Our Lord was not a rule-breaker because he healed on the Sabbath. Jesus got this way of doing things from his Father in heaven. His Father was only about love. Even in his law, God the Father gave it for the benefit for people to live simple and peaceful lives. On the other hand, the Pharisees had laws that weighed people down with unnecessary rules and customs.

God the Father sent Jesus to free people from burdens and the only way to get this freedom is from love. Jesus is love, and when a sick person came before him, he could only heal him, even if it was on the Sabbath when the custom was to do nothing. When hungry people were before him, he could only feed them. When Jesus was on the cross dying, even though he was innocent and people taunted him, out of love, he could only ask for his Father to forgive them.

As God's beloved children, the only way to start a day is not ask what all do I need to accomplish today, but to ask what can I do that shows love. Again, don't get me wrong, I can't do a day without a to-do list, but they can get life complicated as we over do things to keep up with a world that has its goal to do many things to get as much stuff as possible. Showing love helps things to fall in place better. Love always is the right thing to do and never fails.

Simple ways can lead to a lot of good things, and when done with love and care, it does turn out to be a wonder. Good food, simple joys, and a love that comes from Christ are for everyone.

For the Weathered Wearied

Weather is a mood changer. The refrain in the favorite song of the 70's by the Carpenters, "Rainy days and Mondays always get me down," was right about our feelings changing with the weather. I was taking a walk on the beach and passing another walker, she said, "It's a beautiful evening-isn't it? Enjoy your walk." "Yes, it is. I just took a picture of the sunset. Would you like to see it?" Our short conversation was pleasant, and the walk was meditative and peaceful.

That night Lake Michigan was like a plate of glass, but there're times when it can roar. Not to bring up last winter again-during most winters I can bundle up and still take walks, but last winter I had to turn around and go back home because the winds were so frigid. I felt like I lost a good friend that I could not take my beloved walks.

In any coffee shop in America on any morning, people are drinking coffee and talking about the weather. Weather affects our lives-sometimes in horrific ways. On a farm where there is a drought, the family comes together and prays for rain. Or after a tornado strikes a neighborhood, people encourage one another to go on. Storms out in the sea have made sailor's wives widows, and most harbors have memorials to these lost seamen. Floods can move a whole town down river, and people look to the sky for an opening in the dark clouds knowing God is behind there somewhere.

We compare life to weather. "I am going through a storm right now." Then a friend says, "Remember all storms pass." Or we say, "The winds of change are blowing." We have times when we can just feel that something different is going to happen. Seasons also tell us about life. If we are in the "autumn" of our lives, we are getting older. Winter often gets a bad reputation as being used as an analogy for death, but it's not all bad-nothing is purer than a fresh blanket of snow. Spring is the season of renewal with flowers breaking through the crusted ground. I like the idea that seasons change and so will a life. Nothing ever stays the same, and that can be comforting when it seems I stuck in difficult circumstances.

Weather is a circumstance. One day showers come down all day, and on another day it is bright and warm. We grab our umbrella or our sunglasses. Then, the weather changes, and we prepare ourselves for whatever nature has for us. Other circumstances come our way, too. A flat tire is a circumstance, and first seeing it, I can get frustrated in a second. Losing a loved one, getting hours cut at work, having tests come back that show surgery is needed, or an ongoing conflict with a family member that does not seem to be resolving are serious times, but they are all circumstances.

Not to minimize these times, for they are difficult and do break our hearts, but they are all situations like the weather and will change. As clouds blow in on any day and pass through, all our circumstances go through phases like a developing storm. Failure happens, and will happen often many times before success. Grief is a process, and often with a life of its own.

The weather and our circumstances are not what can bring us down. They come in all kinds of forms to test us. What brings us down is our own self-created despair. When we do not look to God for hope that is when we can get down and stay lost.

Another song about weather has a line, "I can see clearly now that the rain had gone." When we are in our circumstances, God gives us choices by his grace. We can see the situation has a dead-end, or we can see it with hope and a new beginning. God has made us to be forward moving people.

When it comes to anything about life from the weather to our situations, we can talk about them, pray about them, curse them, and bless them. In any day, I do all of them. I am so thankful that I have a God who has steadfast love for me, and I can see that everything is a blessing to me as all will work out for the good if I stay faithful. Weather will be weather, and situations will be situations, but God's mercies are new every morning, and I can move forward by God's grace with hope-no matter the weather and circumstance.

Can't Google Love

We can Google anything and get pages of hits. All day long we can search any subject and grow in knowledge. With our noses in our phones and tablets, all kinds of information is available to us. In moments, we can appear to be scientists, connoisseurs, specialists, or scholars. Whatever we want to know we can find out about it by using the right keyword.

One of the ideas that we have these days is that knowledge is power. The one who knows the most "wins." Having the pertinent facts and statistics gives a person an edge over the person who does not have them. The world is very competitive and even the smallest amount of information could be the piece that gives a side in an argument the advantage.

In The Great Debaters, Denzel Washington plays an English teacher for a college for black students during the depression era. Also, he is the coach for the debate team and his goal for the team is to debate Harvard. At his home where the tryouts for the team take place, he draws a circle with chalk on the floor and calls it the "Hot Spot." He challenges the students to enter the circle at their own risk to try and make the team. With that challenge, he says, "Debate is blood sport, and your weapons are words."

This country was founded on debate, and the freedom of speech is one of our greatest assets. But we could also say that politicians and the media use manipulation to try to get their points across to the public. What is most important today is for one side of an issue to say that they are right and that the other side is just loaded with misinformation.

As a kid, I loved to read. I loved mystery novels and would read one a day during the summer because imagining that I was in the story going after bad guys was much more exciting than anything to do on a hot day in the dull suburbs. A trip to the library was an adventure. In books there were far way places and all kinds of characters from pirates to real heroes who made great discoveries and changes in the world. But I would get a little frustrated as I did not know what book to pick up next. The shelves held many books, and I knew I could not possibly read them all.

Reading did give me a curiosity about the world, and I have spent much of my adult life in pursuit of adventures. I have things I want to do before I die. It has been my ambition to have a fulfilling life, but after I have done many things, I have found that there is always more to do, and like when I was in the library, I get frustrated with knowing that there is so much in the world that I will not be able to connect with.

Lately, I have been going in a different direction in my pursuit of knowledge. Getting filled with knowledge is a noble thing to do, but knowing everything is an impossible task. But I did not like the emptiness thinking I was missing out on something. So what do I need to do to be a whole person?

Information can be looked up, but the things we need to have to be a whole person can only be obtained by our own experiences and what we make of them. We have choices on how we think about our lives and how our inner selves shape us of who we are and what we do.

Back in New Testament times, it was very important to have knowledge and to be a good speaker. Traveling teachers would give instruction about how to be a great orator. St Paul was a very intelligent man and a great speaker. As a Roman citizen he had many privileges and one of them was an excellent education. Some people confused St Paul as he went about preaching the Gospel as one of these teachers. Paul wrote that he was not one of these teachers and that the gospel did not have any need for eloquent language.

As St Paul was a well-read person, he talked about how knowledge only puffs us up with arrogance whereas love builds us up to be good people.

And well, yes, we can Google "love." I did Google "love" and got dictionary meanings. Love songs and movies about love came up. Many articles on what philosophers have said about love and all kinds of religious interpretations on love came up, too. Within hours of reading, I could become a "love guru."

But if we want to be a whole person, it has to be more than what we put in our heads and what we do with our lives. When it comes to being whole and true, it comes down to what we believe about ourselves and all that is around us. Or in one word it is about "faith."

St Paul says he knows one thing, "Christ and him crucified." We know we are loved by God, and this love is so great that God gave his one and only Son to live and die for us, and in all that Christ has done, we have a complete life.

When growing through a difficult time, what do we want from another person? Do we want answers or do we want a hug? I suppose I would like both, a hug for comfort and answers to my problems. And as God's beloved child, I do have both at all times. No matter what the situation is, God's love is always by us and in us.

So let's go out for a cup of coffee and share what is in our minds and hearts, and we will find love that is special and that kind of love can't be googled.

Willful Blindness

Scrooge had a point. When he was asked to donate to a charity to help the poor, he asked if the poorhouses were no longer in operation. He was assured that they were. His taxes were paying to help those who needed it, so he did not see why he should give more. The argument was that the help that the government provided was not very adequate, but Scrooge did have a point that the poor were being taken care of in some way.

Scrooge was a fair and honest business man and responsible citizen. His nephew liked him enough to come and visit him on occasion. He did not cheat anyone, and he paid Bob Crachet a low modest wage, but it was still a sum that provided for his family. Scrooge did not know Tiny Tim was sick. If he had known, he might have provided a minimal health plan.

No doubt Scrooge was a bitter old soul, and he did not have a cheerful charitable heart, but he was not a bad man, either. Maybe we could say he was against the growing trend of the commercialism of Christmas.

Scrooge may even have been a church goer. It was the norm back then to go to church. He did believe in Christmas, even with all of his "Bah Humbugs." I can see old Scrooge sitting in a back pew with his arms staunchly folded, and when the offering plate came around, he dropped his tithe in with a frown doubting that the church was going to use it for prudent purposes.

As the story goes with the three visits of the ghosts, Scrooge sees that he needs to open up his heart and to use his wealth to help others. He finds out that giving to others can actually make a person happy. It is more blessed to give than to receive-God loves a cheerful giver-we all love a kind and charitable person.

I was watching a documentary that opened with example in one small town where people were getting sick for what seemed mysterious reasons. One of the town's people investigated and found it was from the drinking water. Upon further investigation, it was that the water was being contaminated from the local factory.

When all this came out, the person who made the discoveries assumed that she would get the whole town behind her to get the factory to stop polluting the river, but she got a disappointing surprise. The town barely would admit that the factory was contaminating their water that was making them sick. They did not want to fully admit that the factory was the culprit because the factory was where most of the town worked and got paid, which gave them their livelihood. They willfully turned their eyes from the problem.

Willful blindness is knowing about a problem but intentionally not seeing it. Watching and reading the news is like living in a goldfish bowl. From my goldfish bowl, I see other people in their goldfish bowls. I can see the problems and the needs of others, but since I am in my bowl, I cannot go to their bowls to help if they need it. I am content to stay in my self-imposed boundaries. Jumping out of my goldfish bowl would take risks, and I am not sure if I want to take that chance for I might get hurt, even if it means helping others.

I said Scrooge had a point-I did not say he was totally right. He did care that the poor had help although it was not very good help. The townspeople had a point about the factory and their paychecks, but people would keep getting sick. I think I have a point in my own life. I am far from rich, and after I pay taxes and give to the church, I do not have much left to give to charity. This applies to my time as well. In any day, I only have so much time to do the things I have to do on my to-do-list, and when asked to give and do more, I am overwhelmed and want to say, "Bah Humbug." I can come up with a lot of excuses, which to my mind are good reasons, not to help others in need.

The world is a big place with a lot of people with many having a lot of need. Every day we hear about issues and causes, and it can be very difficult to discern what to do.

With so many needs, it would be easy to turn away from all of them and be content in my little goldfish bowl, but that would not be right. Christians are engaged with others, especially those with needs. To struggle with the needs of the world and to have some heartache about them is a good thing. The feelings we have for others say that we have compassion.

Jesus was about to go on a prayer retreat when he saw that a crowd was following him. He had compassion for them and turned back to teach them about the kingdom of God, and he also provided the crowd with a meal. Jesus did so many things like healing that John says at the end of His book that it would be impossible to write them all down.

Still, Jesus did not go to all places in the world and teach and heal everyone. He stayed in a very small geographical area. Later, He sent His disciples out into areas of the world to heal and teach.

We are those disciples who are to get out and help those in need and to teach about God's kingdom. As one person this can be overwhelming. I am only one person, but I am a citizen of many citizens and a church member of many church members. Always first, I need to be a charitable person and be kind to all those I meet in a day. Being kind to all others is a no-brainer for Christians. And then, together we see, listen, and work to fight the injustices of this world that cause so many needs for people.

An Untimed God

Cell phone time is very accurate, but I find that I am always digging in my pocket to check the time. For me, I like my wrist watch. I can flip my wrist, and the time is right there. Checking the time frequently is a habit with me, maybe a bad habit. When it comes to scheduling and getting things done, I'm about as OCD as a person can get.

Getting through a day is all about timing. A productive day is about having the to-do-list and the clock match-up. It's like a major league hitter who only has a fraction of a second to react to the ball when it leaves the pitcher's hand to when it soars to the plate. If a hitter is off in his timing, he will get in a slump, and he's back to the minors.

For years I tried to get everything in place, but the more I worked to get it all done, it seemed that I was fighting it all. On my to-do-list, there were plenty of check marks that things were getting done on schedule. Yet, I was not feeling as whole as I thought I would be feeling with my accomplishments.

Life was working well, but I still thought that I was not right. And I found that it all had to do with my timing.

I was working and pushing to get things done. When something did not go as planned, I became frustrated, and I also took it very personally-like I failed in some way.

Being helpless in a situation was not a very comfortable feeling. If something went wrong with a project, I took it as that I was not prepared. My philosophy was, "Those who are prepared can anticipate the things that can go wrong." All can go perfect if I am organized, so I blamed myself if anything went wrong.

When the timing was all off, I got into these moments of self-pity. "But I work so hard!" I can throw the best pity parties where I think that I am the only one in the world with troubles. I figure that I work so hard that I did not deserve anything bad to happen to me.

We might ask, "Why did this happen to me." But I know that life has its difficult times. We can expect trials to test us to see if we are genuine people of perseverance. Okay, things can go wrong, but things need to go wrong on time. When some wrong was untimely, I found that I was asking, "Why did this have to happen, NOW?" I have so much to do and so little time to begin with.

Feeling sorry for oneself is a very vulnerable spot. The place of misery where one feels defeated because life is not going the way that he would like is a very weak spot and is open to all kinds of problems. When we are felling unhappy about ourselves and our situations, we might just do about anything to start feeling in control again. This way of getting back in control can lead to addictive behavior and can be very destructive.

It took years to figure this out, and I am still working on it. In talking with my friend, Sam, we hit upon something that has got me thinking every day. Sam told me about a phrase that he heard in a bible study about God being "An Untimed God." He said the discussion was around the topic about how our plans do not always turn out how we would like. God seems to have His timing that lets unexpected things to drop down on us.

Like a flat tire in pouring rain or getting the flu just when we have a lot to get done. Or in a marriage where two people do try to get together, but the timing never seems right. One person is tired and the other person wants to talk.

Sam told me that the group talked about how God as eternally divine does not see time as we do. They imagined what eternity must be like. Seconds and years are all alike to God. For His plans, He can do whatever He thinks is best with not much of a time schedule. If God thinks it will take forty years to wander in the wilderness for a trip that needs only to take weeks, then He is okay with that.

But God's timing was just right when He sent his Son in the world to save us from sin. At the right time He sent Jesus to be born for us, to live and die for us. Then on the third day he rose for us, so we have life now and forever.

God's timing is about love. Life is not about getting the most accomplishments, but it is about love. Love connects us to all things. Although life can seem chaotic and crazy, no matter what happens and when it happens, we can still always move forward in love.

I'm still a clock watcher, but I try not to get trapped in my schedule. All that I need to get done can seem overwhelming at times, but all that needs to be done and when it gets done is all done in God's time. So when I am tested with untimely surprises, I do my best to live by faith and the grace of God.

And I'm free when I trust that God is working out all the timing for me. Things happen in His time, and since He is eternal, there is always plenty of time, and there is always enough grace at every moment to live a life where all gets in place in God's time.

What to Do with a Life

I come from a large family with more cousins than the Hatfields and the McCoys put together. So when June comes along, I am usually going to a lot of graduations. What's ironic to me after sitting through many graduation speeches by young people so full of aspirations, I am not more hopeful. I'm not inspired. I guess as I'm getting up there in years I've gotten a little cynical.

Most of the speeches are about going out and changing the world. But it does not seem that the world wants to do much changing. Today's news report another mass shooting at a school, more scandals heating up in Washington, and peace negotiations have failed again in the Middle East.

One speech was not very good, for it came off very badly. It was not that the young lady was not well poised. She was very well spoken, and she had a good theme. But her examples just did not make it. She talked about how when the class was young that they wanted to grow up and become their favorite superheroes. But then they got older and wanted to become teachers and firemen. Now as high school graduates, they want to become doctors and lawyers.

I wanted to shout, "Wait a second! What's so bad about being a teacher or fireman? And how many of the graduates are planning to be doctors and lawyers?" But I think I got her point. She was trying to make it real. As young people think about what they want to do with a life, the best thing is to want to reach your true potential. My thought is that any job done well contributes to the good of the whole.

I read a study about jobs for graduates that no president in the past one hundred years has created enough jobs to keep up with population growth. And the world is changing so quickly that many jobs have not even been invented yet for a young person even to dream about. Finding a sustainable income is getting tougher.

For my graduation speech, I would not so much talk about on what we are to do but more about how we are to go about doing things. I am all for discovering and using our talents. What is most important is that we are good people in all that we do.

Here is the problem. What is good? My speech would need to define what "good" is. Being productive and going out to change the world can mean many things. Today, suicide bombers are thinking they are doing a good thing by taking out a bunch of people.

In my speech, my definition of "good" would have to come from the church. In the church we hear God speak to us from His Word. This Word tells us to taste the Word. It is like eating fine food and in the food we are to see that our Lord is good. When God created the earth, sun, moon, stars, and every living thing, God said about each thing, "It is good."

As young people struggle to find what they are to do with their lives, the only place they can know what to and how to do it is from the church. Unfortunately, many young people have grown quite skeptical of anything with authority. They should expect parents, schools, and government to keep them safe. But many young people are not safe even in their own homes as parents are abusive or don't provide regular routines of dinner time, homework time, and bed time. Where can young people go to find love and care?

I am willing to say that young people are on the fringes of society. What I mean is that they are looking for places to fit in. To say that being lost is not a bad thing because in the search for the places to belong they find out who they really are. But they do need support as they go through this time of discovery.

No matter our age and circumstances we need love and care. And the love and care we get in church from God in His Word is like no other. In the love of Christ, we are restored, supported, and given a firm foundation.

The hard reality of the church is that it can come across as one of those places of authority that people do not trust. Often, I hear from young people that the church is full of hard people and hypocrites. Scandal does rock the church, and when the church is good, it is good, but when it is bad, it is bad.

We who are the church have to roll up our sleeves and be Jesus' feet and share Him with a skeptical and hurting world. God gives us His steadfast love. Most people are in tough circumstances. Some of the hard stuff comes from our messes that are our own faults, and we have to suffer the consequences. Or some difficult things just come our way because we live in a sinful world.

What the church does not need to do is solve all the problems-maybe we can help out with some relief, but what we can do is to help people see the Lord's steadfast love, and they will get through each step of their days by the grace of God.

When I started out preaching, a retired pastor said every sermon is telling people to get a life. It is good to ask every day, "Lord, what am I to do with this life?" The answer that we should be hearing from the church is, "Have a life in my Son, Jesus Christ." This life is a good life, with all things working out by God's grace. Now, I'm hopeful for young people and for us all at any age.

I'm Here Most Fridays

"Now, I work every Tuesday, Wednesday, and Saturday, and I'm here most Fridays," said Adriane, "Sometimes I have to take Fridays off because I can't afford the day care for my three year old daughter." I stop off for coffee every morning and Adriane has a big smile, and I thought she was a new waitress, but she has been at the diner for several months. Her shift was changed. "Yea, it's a little better, my mom with her schedule can watch my daughter but still not on Fridays. Between what daycare costs and what I make, it's rough."

On my way to work I got to thinking about a vacation in Florida when we were all kids. We had a green station wagon with simulated wood door panels, and our dad drove us all down from Chicago to the Keys for two weeks. My older brother and I were big eaters, and with two younger sisters, we ate a lot of tuna fish sandwiches and cereal sitting on the back gate of the wagon at rest stops. But every day we ate one meal in a restaurant, and one time we had this nice young waitress, and she was real good, but I remember her stopping and forlornly looking out the window at the ocean. She said, "My six year old son is going fishing today with his sitter." As a mother and a waitress herself, my mom listened to her tell about how she was a single mom and was nervous about him going, but the sitter was really reliable. Back then I can't remember what the bill was for lunch for four kids and two adults, but my mom left the waitress a dollar, which was a good tip back then for any meal.

Tips can be lean or good. I thought about Adriane and day care costs. I've heard from many waitresses through the years say about half way through their shift, "Well, I just about broke even." It's almost a gamble whether or not a day at work will bring in some money or be a loss.

The old song from James Taylor comes back to me from time to time, "Winter, spring, summer and fall, all you have to do is call, and I will be there, you've got a friend." I have always liked this song where we know that there is another person out there willing to meet us where we are at. This maybe does not rhyme as well as what James Taylor sings, but Scripture tells us that we have a high priest who is there for us.

In Old Testament times a high priest spoke for the people. The priest was able to go before God and represent the needs of the people. He served as a mediator, and in his speaking, he told God what the circumstances of the people and would ask for God's help. As a representative of the people, it would be necessary that the priest knew everything about every situation of the people. The priest lived among the people and knew what they were going through because he himself was going through these things.

Many places in Scripture like Psalm 110 and Hebrews talk about how Christ is the perfect high priest. No one can know the people so well and can be the perfect mediator between God and people other than Jesus. As the Son of God, Jesus knows the Father very well as they are one, and as completely human, he knows what it is like to live a life in this world.

Jesus was tempted though he did not sin. We are tempted and do sin, but we need to remember that we have the same power as Jesus has to fight these temptations. Jesus used the Word of God to fight, and we have that same Word with us today in our battles. When Jesus came to earth to be like us, he burst the limits. He is far away in all parts of the infinite universe and as close to us to live in our hearts.

In Old Testament times the priest offered sacrifices for the sins of the people. Jesus is the perfect high priest because he took all of what we have upon him, and he offered himself as the sacrifice that would please God once and for all times. Now all is right between us and God.

Most of the time we did okay as I remember my mom still in her brown and orange uniform after work at the kitchen table counting out the dimes and quarters and giving me a handful of change to take my bike down to the store for milk and bread. Then, I would go to my drum lessons with all quarters and the teacher liked it because now he had money for tolls.

So now I give a little more in tips to waitresses knowing they need every dollar to pay bills. When I see Adriane, I ask her how she is doing, and on Fridays when I see her, I give her more than usual to help pay for the babysitter. I have seen tough times, too, and we have to be in this together.

I know pretty much where Adriane is coming from, and I remember to say a pray for her as she has asked me to do as our conversations have at times turned to faith. Where else can a conversation go when it comes down to the things we need in life? Faith tells us that in Christ we have a high priest who is perfect and knows our every need. So we turn and pray and can be confident that every word is heard and will be taken care of, even on a Friday when it is looking the tips are going to be just enough to make it.

Getting Ready for Faith's Worst Case Scenario

I was in a class in seminary, and the professor was lecturing on the different approaches to evangelism. The professor all of a sudden broke from his lecture and told a story.

The story was short and did wake me up. He told about a time when he was in another country on a short mission trip and had met a young girl. She had recently converted to Christianity, and he was amazed at how much she knew about the bible being so new to the faith. The country suffered from poor economics and the politics were volatile. Where she was living there were violent clashes, and it seemed the country was on the brink of civil war. Religious freedom was also in jeopardy in all of the changes. When he asked her how her faith was getting her through this time of hard tensions she looked him in the eye with candor and a soft voice of conviction, "I am preparing myself for persecution."

Well, no matter why the professor told this story it has been fixed in my memory and pops up every time I talk about the mission of the church. One of the problems I have with talking about missions is that as Americans, we really don't have to be concerned about persecution. Scripture often talks about how we are to suffer for our faith and to find joy in that suffering. Admittedly, I have never really suffered for my faith. I have suffered because of the lack of faith and have had to go through the consequences of the wrongs I have done. But I have never had to go through any kind of hardship because of my faith in Christ.

Life is Good Today

What a great blessing in this country of religious freedom. We can believe and worship as we please with no fear of persecution. But then I have a question. Are we as Christians in America missing out on the joy of suffering for our faith? When the prophets and disciples went under severe physical hardship, they knew that they were standing their ground and doing God's will. Under this pronouncement from others that they were indeed people of faith and had stood up their beliefs under harsh treatment, they counted it all as joy.

An early Christian under the oppressive rule of the Romans could stand out in public and say, "Jesus is God." People would find this very interesting and might be very accepting of Jesus as the Romans worshipped many gods. But if a Christian stood up and said, "Jesus is my Lord." Then, this person was asking for trouble. For at that time only Nero was considered to be the only Lord and only he was to be worshiped.

We read many accounts in history books where early Christians did suffer atrocities for their faith. And in Scripture, we read of the stoning of Stephen as just one example of what happened when a person stood up for their faith.

It has been said, "If you live for God, you can expect trouble from the world." As I said I have experienced trouble, but it has all been my own fault from the wrong I have done. I have also gone through hard times but even non-believers have problems. But I don't know if I have suffered for my faith. This is a blessing as an American. But will I ever have the joy of suffering for my faith? Is this something I should even be thinking about?

The world seems to be changing quickly, and it is often changing in direct opposition to Christianity. I don't have a crystal ball, but I think it will get worse before it gets better. The world has always rebelled against God' will. Will an American Christian ever face the lions as many early Christians did? I doubt it. But who knows?

We do know that we should be ready for any kind of persecution from ridicule to a worst case scenario of facing death.

St Peter wrote his epistles to prepare these early Christians for the storm of persecution that was ahead of them. His purpose in his letters was to help Christians to live a Christ-like life in a hostile world and to know how to handle persecution as Christ did.

Here is a short list of what Christians should be keeping in mind and heart as we live in a culture that often is contrary to what we believe:

- **Be certain Jesus is Lord of our lives.** Make sure that all we do is from God and not from a world view.
- **Always be prepared.** Know God's word will and be ready to give a defense.
- **Be focused.** Keep the discussion on Christ and always finish with the cross and the gift of life for now and forever. Be friendly and uplifting and not pushy or arrogant. Keep it simple and don't get bogged down or sidetracked on irrelevant details.
- **Be looking for opportunities.** As followers of Christ, our main purpose is to spread the good news of salvation. Don't be looking for a fight but be open to a conflict as a chance to tell about Christ.

I have always felt safe as a Christian living in America, maybe too safe. Am I feeling secure because I have been hiding my values when they are contrary to a growing popular worldly view? Maybe I am not as bold with what I believe because I don't feel strong enough to face persecution, even if it is only some hard criticism. So I have lots of questions that ask if I have a strong enough faith to face any kind of persecution that comes my way. I hope the answer is that I have a faith that is ready.

God's Pat on the Back

I have to admit after a job well done, I like a pat on the back. It is very rewarding. Recognition by our peers is very pleasing and beneficial. Knowing that we have done well, we are motivated to keep going with more effort to do good work.

So when someone shouts out at me, "Hey Tom, you sure did a great job," that affirmation with a pat on the back is something that makes me want to keep going in a positive direction.

Several years ago when I was giving piano lessons, after a student completed a lesson in the book, I had a bunch of stickers that said things like "Hooray! You did awesome." The students could pick a sticker to put on the page. Then, when all the pages had stickers on them, the student moved on to the next level. Twice a year, I had recitals and at the end of the recital, each student received a small trophy with the name of the song on a little plaque. The purpose was for the students to collect the trophies, so they could see how practice was moving them forward from their early songs to more advanced pieces.

On our shelves and in scrapbooks, we have our awards, diplomas, blue ribbons, newspaper clippings, and certifications. They are good for us to see what we have done. If we succeeded once, we can be successful again.

But as much as I believe in pats on the back for motivation to do good work, the fact is that we will not always get recognition for jobs well done. Others don't always see the work that goes on behind the scenes. We may put a lot of time and effort into something, and it's not fully appreciated for what it is.

Some work is just "thankless." But we do the work anyway. Whether or not we have a nice boss or a grouch who never has a good word for us, we do our work as best as we can. The best thing we can do is to give ourselves pats on the back. We need to be our own best friend and tell ourselves that we are doing okay.

To be sure, I am not saying that we need to keep feeding our own egos with our own self-praise. How good we feel about ourselves is not dependent on what others say or think about us.

This is where our faiths turn things upside down about ego and self-esteem. Faith has its own unique way of looking at what we do as God's people and how we feel about it. When it comes down to good work, we have to admit that all that we have and what we do comes from God, and He alone deserves the glory and praise.

As we know that our good works only come from God's help, what we have to understand also about the good that we do has a totally different kind of reward system than we get from our earthly accomplishments. God gives us pats on the back, but they are not at all like getting an outstanding citizen's award from a community organization.

Some will love us when we talk of Christ as the way to heaven and the gift of eternal life, but others will hate us for it and want to do us harm. This is where it really gets weird for us as Christians. The hurt done to us is God's pat on the back. When we are suffering because of our faith, we can be certain then that we are doing God's good work and that He is pleased with us.

It is not at all easy being a Christian, and for the most part it is also not very simple. Standing up for what one believes often means sacrifice. Living a life that is full of conviction for the Lord often comes with trials. Many times we will feel like we are hanging by a thin limb. That hanging by a limb is God's test to see if our faith is real and genuine. Life as a Christian is different from a life that is in the world. And if we are living differently others will notice and may abandoned us. Although we are left feeling we are hanging by a limb, we remember it is God's limb, and it is quite strong.

St. Paul experienced many hardships on his mission trips. He went through shipwrecks, was beaten, endured starvation, and spent time in prison for the sake of the Gospel, but he considered it a joy to suffer this way for the purpose of spreading the good news of Christ.

Life is Good Today

After Christ's ascension, the disciples were continuing Jesus' message of the kingdom of God. When religious leaders started hearing the disciples' message was the same of Jesus', they feared that they, too, may incite the crowds to rebelling against them as they thought Jesus had done. So the leaders had the disciples beaten thinking that this would discourage them. But the disciples only saw this "punishment" as joy as they knew they were suffering for the sake of the good news of Christ.

As Americans in a free society, our freedom to worship as we please is a blessing, but we have to admit that this country is changing quickly. Many values of today's culture run contrary to Christian beliefs. Some people may hate us for our values, but we are to be bold and stand for what we believe. Not that we go looking for an argument, but in our daily lives, we can proclaim the good news and live a Christian life with boldness. And if we do suffer in some way, we count it as joy knowing that this is God's way of giving us a pat on the back for living a life that proclaims Christ in all that we say and do.

A No-Nonsense God

Recently, I was channel surfing and stopped on a cable news station, and there was a discussion going on about the continuing violence in our cities. In my own mind, I have come to the conclusion that we do have a breakdown in our culture. From what I was picking up on in the discussion was that there is a declining respect for authority. As I just got in the middle of the discussion that seemed to be turning into a debate when one of the panelists said, "We are getting away from God and His ways." This prompted another panelist to say, "But it does not make sense for our world today to follow the outmoded ways of a dictatorial God."

The host was pushing to sum the discussion up for a commercial break, but I wanted to hear more about what the one panelist meant by a "dictatorial God." It sounded like a harsh way to describe God. Just to be sure I got the meaning correct, I looked up "dictatorial." I was right. It means that someone imposes their mind and will on people under them.

The big word here is "imposes." Everyone has a mind and will, and it's okay to say what that is, but no one likes to be forced to do something and coercion hardly ever brings long term benefits.

God definitely has His own mind and will. He has given all of humanity His Law, but He has also given us free will. We can choose to do the will of God or to go against it.

Free will is not that difficult of a concept to understand, but somehow we just can't get it, especially when something goes wrong. We like to blame others when things go wrong, and then things get real messy in our relationships.

God gave us free will all the way in the Garden of Eden when He first created everything. God did not want to force His created beings to obey His will, which He meant for the benefit of their lives. In the very beginning, God gave only one simple instruction. Adam and Eve could eat from any of the trees except one. If they ate of it, they would know about good and evil. Up until now they only knew what is good. Doesn't that sound like a nice plan from God? Humans would only know good, but they also had the choice if they wanted to know evil. This does not sound like a dictatorial God. I think God is being open and fair.

The first two humans had a relationship with God and knew Him as kind and loving, but they wanted more out of paradise. Just think about it, they didn't have to work at all for food and clothing.

But all of that good flew out the window one day when they decided that they wanted more than perfection. We are never really content with what we have. Admittedly, we want things to always to go our way, even if that way is not the best for us. God knows what is right for us. He is righteous. Only God knows perfectly what is right and wrong. If we listen to Him, we can do well.

But we lost that perfect goodness when Adam and Eve sinned. The fall into sin and all of its consequences is our inheritance. God is no-nonsense when it comes to His beloved creation. He meant what He said and now humans have to do sweaty work and suffer death. As I said God is righteous, and He can't wink at sin. God really wanted things to go perfectly well, but human disobedience needed to be punished. Now, Adam and Eve needed to be tossed out of paradise and suffer all the pains of being human, even death.

This is all very fair. God told Adam and Eve exactly what would happen if they did not follow His will for them. God is righteous and just, but we also need to know God is good and very loving. For the problem of sin and death, God provided a solution.

Out of His love right there in the garden, God made a promise that there would be a Savior. As much as God is no-nonsense about His will and justice, God is no-nonsense about His promises to restore humans to a right relationship with Him.

God kept the promise by sending His own Son, Jesus, to take the punishment of death for the world on the cross where he suffered and died.

Because of what Jesus did, we will die, but we will die not an eternal death. Now, we will live eternally with God in heaven.

This gift of eternal life is ours by faith. It's very important that we know it is only by faith. We can't work ourselves into heaven. Jesus has done all the work for us by His death and resurrection.

Although we do get all we have from God as a gift, we are to be no-nonsense about it all. When we do sin, we are to be sincere and repent of those sins.

With faith we are to see and hear all that God has for us. Living by faith, is the best life where we are following the will of God and trusting that His ways are the only way to live.

Most people do not understand God's will. God tells us this that His ways are not our ways. Just because we do not understand His will for us, this does not mean we do not follow His will. Faith tells us to trust our God who is righteous and just, but we remember He is also full of love for us. We really can't even comprehend how much God loves us, but He is totally no-nonsense about His love for us, and we know it when we look at Jesus.

Basking in Peace

If you're a person who sleeps like a rock every night, I envy you. I'm not a very good sleeper. On most nights, it takes me some time to fall asleep, and then I'm up several times during the night walking the floors trying to wear myself out. I toss and turn so much that my bed in the morning looks like there was a wrestling match in it all night.

I think one of the reasons why I don't sleep well is that I can't seem to turn my mind off. All of the day's events are running through my mind like a merry-go-round with its lever stuck in the on position.

I'm anxious most of the time because I am one of those people who takes on other people's pain. I have a tough time watching the news as I see hurt, suffering, and chaos in the world. I want to find solutions for those who are having any kind of hardship. But I know there are no easy answers that work like silver bullets, for the problems are often complex.

I am like the beauty contestant during the questioning part of the pageant. The contestant is asked, "If there is one thing you would like to accomplish if you were named queen, what would that be?" After a second of pressured thought, she says with bright eyes and a wide smile, "I would like to work for world peace." The crowd gives great applause, and the judges give her high marks for such a grand and noble answer.

We want world peace. Especially at times like Christmas, we look for peace and try to have it all around us. Although we see conflict around us, Christmas brings peace. There was the Christmas truce of 1914 when

British and German soldiers put down their weapons and shared seasonal greetings. But the truce did not last and the war continued for more years.

Last century, there was WWI, WWII, the Korean War, Vietnam, and the Gulf War. This century begins with wide acts of terrorism. Looking at a globe, we can point to many hotspots.

Living in the city we hear sirens going throughout the day and night. Each siren says there is some kind of trouble. I have a friend who stops and says a prayer every time he hears a siren knowing that someone is in need of help.

The thing is about peace is that it's just not going to happen. I'm not a history buff, but I do know that complete peace in the world has never happened and my guess it will never happen. Don't get me wrong. I am all with the beauty contestant and think that we should work for peace. We need to work at peace in our families, communities, workplaces, schools, and countries. But conflict is inevitable.

Since Adam blamed Eve for the fall into sin, the world is made up of sinful humans who have had conflict. It wasn't long before their two sons had problems, and one killed the other. Sin is like throwing bombs that sabotage any peaceful situation. When one person gains something, someone else loses. The world just works that way, and that at times can cause conflict.

The thing about conflict resolution is that it can still keep me up at night as I try to work out problems even if the problem is my own selfish ego. This is not a bad thing if I spend some time trying to get over my ego and work out the conflict. We should be taking time to solve any problem even if it we have to keep going over it. I wonder what would happen in the world if kings, presidents, and prime ministers all gave a tireless altruistic try at bringing peace to the world.

So far I have talked about peace being the absence of conflict, and I have also said conflict will always happen. At our best, we can work out conflicts, but that does not stop conflict from beginning. All it takes is a small sliver of sin to get into me, and I am in conflict.

What would it be like if we had peace even if there was conflict? We often think that peace is the absence of conflict. But by faith we can have peace even in the most horrific of times. We have peace because the conflict caused by our sin between us and God has been settled by Jesus when he took our punishment for our sins on the cross. Now that the big problem of sin is over we have peace. In a world of conflict, it may seem that any kind of peace is hard to understand. But the peace of God is so deep and profound that is beyond human understanding. This peace can only come by faith.

On those sleepless nights, sometimes I think I am prince of the cynics and think that peace will never happen in many situations. Yet, afflictions can be a time to turn to God. We find that God is meeting our needs like a flower opening its petals in spring. Soon we see that we are basking in God's peace. By faith, we have peace that is bountiful and complete, and this is the peace we bring to all of our hectic days and restless nights.

By faith we trust that God will provide for us in every situation-no matter how difficult the conflict is. For me, trust is saying before I go to bed, "All is in God's hand. Peace is here." I can shut off the worries and problems and know all will work out to God's good plan. This gives me an inner calm. Now, I can send the prize fighter home whom I hired to knock me out at bedtime and fall asleep in peace.

Empathizing Empathy

In a busy world that often seems on the verge of chaos, and as an adult trying to make it all work while getting along with others in this crazy world, I need to do my best to keep my cool in tough situations. If I am upset about something like someone cutting me off in heavy traffic, I maybe short on patience and lash out at the rude driver.

My first thought is that I wish I had the Batmobile with rockets to fire at the guy. What is needed is that I flip the situation around and put my shoes on the receiving end of my response. Although the situation is tense, I can make it better by doing something that will be received as I would like to receive it. No matter the situation I never like to be dealt with in a disrespectful way.

Pretty basic stuff-right? We have been taught this since we were kids. It's all kind of "golden rule" type stuff, but taking the time to turn a situation around and seeing it all from another's perspective takes a developed mature attitude of deep care.

At church, a lot of sermons have to do with the way we treat others. Empathizing empathy is a key to a Christ-like life. The more that I try to put myself in other people's shoes the more I can be helpful to others.

We are all human and go through the basic things in life. We all have the same emotions. We know what it is like to be frustrated, sad, angry, and disappointed. We all have had situations go terribly wrong and have suffered losses of some kind. When we share with each other that our lives can be tough, we have a good idea what each other is talking about.

Life is Good Today

Empathy is like a rain shower. We do not have to go under every drop of the shower to get wet. As in the experiences of life, we don't have to have every experience to have a good idea what life is about. Each of us have experienced enough about life, so we can have empathy for others and do our best to help others. What we can do is try to learn about the world as much as we can. In our learning, we can at least open ourselves to what others have gone through and hear what they have to say.

With an opened mind I may still not agree with what they are saying. But I can now respond with my own ideas that have been tested, and I am confident that what I believe is true. When I share what I believe, I can say it with love and hope it is received with the good intentions that I want it to be.

What I mean is that empathy is necessary, but it can get complicated in a very diverse world. I may put myself in another's shoes, but sometimes I find that I disagree with where that person is coming from. Empathy does not mean that we all get on the same page.

In our culture, we have a tendency to over emphasize empathy. We think that we have to accept all the ideas of others. But it may just so happen that after we try to understand another person, we have to make a judgement if we agree with that person or not. It is okay to say to another person that his or her way of thinking and believing is different from your own.

To understand and to put empathy into practice, we have a perfect example of care for others in Jesus. God sent Jesus down to earth to dwell among us to live like us in every way. Maybe it is difficult to think of our Lord and Savior as a baby who had dirty diapers and cried when he was hungry. While growing up, he played with other kids and probably went home with skinned knees. Jesus laughed and cried. Although he never did sin, he was tempted in every way. With the Pharisees, Jesus faced conflict and was direct with them, even if it meant knowing how they would plot against him and that on one day they would put him to death. When Jesus was with the crowds, he had compassion on them and met them at their needs. He fed them, healed them of their diseases, casted out demons, and taught them about the kingdom of God, so they could have strong faiths.

Jesus' whole purpose is to show that God, his Father, who is high above us in heaven is also close to us. Jesus is God in the flesh, so he could live for us and die for us. Jesus lived just like us, and he died for us by going to the cross to take the punishment for our sins.

By his love for us, Jesus took on all of our infirmities. Jesus was willing to do it all for us, and he did it all for us. By his dying and rising, Jesus defeated all that can hurt us. We are forgiven and free.

In this freedom we can help others in their situations. Sometimes the situations get really serious.

Recently, a police officer in our community was shot and killed as he pursued an armed robber. The robber turned and shot the officer in the head. The officer was one month away from retiring after thirty –three years of service. I could not imagine the sorrow that his wife and children had, but not imagining did not stop us from doing our best to support the family.

For this family, we know that Jesus is there for them. Nothing can get by Jesus, for he knows how we feel in every situation. From Jesus' heart, he comes to each of our hearts in the deepest way, so he is always a true help to us.

Happiness When "Blank" Happens

Recently, I went through a kind of mid-life crisis. I say a kind of mid-life crisis because according to a friend when I told him about it, he said, "Tom, you're way past fifty, you're too old to be having a mid-life crisis. You should have had it years ago." Well, years ago, I was too busy taking care of a home, working, and raising my son as a single dad.

Although it was all challenging, I was having the best time of my life, but now with all of my landscaping projects pretty much done and my son away at college and no more helping with homework and going to baseball games, I have had time to think about what I am going to do with the rest of my life. I felt like my life was stalled like an old beat up car.

We don't know how much time we've got, so I started to make a bucket list. You know the things a person wants to do before he kicks the bucket. For my list, I made up a statement with a blank: I will be happy when _____ happens. As I tried to fill in the blanks, that's when I felt a crisis wanting to kick-in.

I was feeling a hole inside in of me as my life was going through some obvious changes. I'm a nurturing type of guy. I need to care for something. I thought of buying a goldfish.

The whole problem is that I have set myself up by making up a fill-in-the-blank statement that only could lead me to gloom and doom. For most of my life, it seems I've been waiting for stuff to happen. Getting my first bike, then my first car, and graduating high school, college, and I knew everything would come together with my getting a Master's degree for the dream job that I always desired. For the most part, my work has gone well, but I hardly ever felt that I was living the dream. Now, I am planning for retirement although still several years away.

At this coffee shop that I go to in the mornings, some retired guys meet there every morning, I have gotten to know them, and one guy told me about a cabin that he bought. It needed a lot of work, but it is on a beautiful lake. He says he figures he will get it to the way he wants it in about twenty years. After a few months of working on the cabin, he started thinking that he maybe he just needs to enjoy it the way it is now.

Another guy said he wanted to do so much in his work and try to accomplish a lot, but he found he was always being interrupted. These interruptions kept him for achieving a lot of his goals. It was not until late in his career that he found that those interruptions were the meaning of his life.

As I was putting my bucket list together, I was finding that life is about more than happy moments and accomplishments.

In talking to the guy with the cabin and the other guy with the interruptions, we got to the point that life has meaning because God is in every moment.

With all of our planning, we really don't know what is going to happen next-do we? That can be scary-not to have control of what situation is coming next. I mean it's peace and comfort that we really want-right? It would be good to have a say in what we think is peace for our situations-sounds good at first-doesn't it?

Look at King David. He went off for a walk in the valley of the shadow of death. Life is about being close to all kinds of bad things. Notice how in Psalm 23 that David while being so close to danger that he does not ask God for anything. He just knew that God is giving him comfort every step of the way.

Don't get me wrong! I know God says we can go to Him. God wants us to seek and ask Him for our needs. But what would happen to our levels of contentment in our difficult situations, even in the most horrific times, if we already knew God is with us with all of his love, power, and glory.

We don't have to wait for stuff to happen to be happy. Faith sees and hears that God forgives us of every sin, gives us all of His love in Jesus, and puts all of God's power and glory in every minute of our lives. All of these things are our peace.

How we can have our best life right now is for our faiths to see and hear all that God is doing for us at this very moment. Although some situations make it seem that life is not going anywhere, God has made us to be forward moving people. We need to understand always that God is with us now and in the next moment whatever that moment is.

I am thinking I have a lot good things a head of me still. I have a few ideas about what I want to do. But I know that my best moment is the one that I am in. And that the next moment is my best moment. That may not make sense, but faith sees and hears all that God is doing for me. If I believe in all who God is and what He does for me in His awesome love, then I am good to go in any moment.

Keeping the Big Picture

While out shopping I bumped into a friend who was head of the psychology department of a community college, he asked, "Hey Tom, I am short a teacher for a grief therapy class. Do you want to teach the class?" I thought for a moment and said, "Yes, I think it will work well."

As a pastor I have counseled many people who were grieving, and also this all seemed very serendipitous to me as I had just several months earlier lost a very close loved one. I got the textbook and started again studying the stages of grief.

In the class we did a lot of sharing of our own personal experiences with grief, and the class, as we learned about grief, turned into a kind of a support group. I remember one student shared as her story mostly sums up the stages we go through when we have suffered a loss. She shared when she discovered her father-in-law's body after he had committed suicide. Her husband and she knew that he was depressed with chronic pain, but they did not ever think he was so depressed that he wanted to take his own life.

She visited her father-in-law every day and brought him a meal. On this day, she walked in the door with her usual, "Hello dad," but she know something was wrong right away when she did not hear him say, "Be right there." Thinking something was wrong, she walked around the house getting more anxious and then found his body in the bathroom.

At the moment she ran out of the house, the neighbor saw her and ran to her seeing that something was terribly wrong. Telling the neighbor what had just happened, the neighbor wanting to calm her down said over and over again, "It's okay, it's okay."

In the class the student said, "Hearing the neighbor say over and over again that it was okay really made me angry because everything was not okay. It was the worst moment of my life."

What brought this story up was that we were talking about how in the big picture of things everything is really okay. When we see life as a matter of living and dying, and we do make it through somehow and are okay.

The discussion we had in class was kind of tense. I tried to make the point that although we never want to minimalize the difficult times we have in life, but we do want to get to the point that we can move forward in life after a loss and know things can be good again.

But we have to admit there is a rub here between the loss of someone dear to us or going through a very difficult time and the time when everything is good again. At the time of loss or trial, we may never think that life can move to a time when we think all is okay.

Early on in ministry I got some advice from a retired pastor, he said, "Always try to keep the big picture in front of your church members." I have tried to keep that advice in my ministry. But first I had to figure out what the big picture is and what were all the little pictures that try to block what we are to focus on as we go on in life.

Heaven has to be the big picture. But as I thought about saying heaven is the big picture, just saying heaven is not enough. We need to feel connected to heaven, but how do we feel connected to something so far away from us as we walk our earthly journey?

That's where all those little things that happen in our lives come in. All of the little things from flat tires in the pouring rain to the washing machine breaking down and flooding the basement can be distractions from thinking about heaven as our goal. Then, we also have those few but heavy things like the loss of a loved one that can bring us down as we go through the grief process of shock and anger.

If we let them, all those little things that happen in a day, and there can be many for any day has good, bad, and ugly things, can take us away from a picture of heaven. Every day is a mix of all kinds of things that can leave us feeling that we are in a whirlwind. Soon we have lost our focus of what life is really about.

But if we live by faith, we can see that every moment is a test of our faiths. All of the things that happen to us are to point us up to heaven.

This lesson of faith seems to have to be learned over and over again throughout life. One woman who is the most faithful person I know suffered the loss of her husband to pancreatic cancer. At the age of eighty she had experienced many things in her life, even living through WWII in Europe. She spent most of her childhood running from bombs and felt true hunger from not eating for days at a time, but she never loss a husband of fifty two years before. As strong as she was, she had to go through the grief process, but all the while she looked to heaven for help.

Looking up to heaven we see our risen and ascended Lord Jesus. We see Him with scars on His hands where He went to the cross to take the punishment for our sins. Now with every sin forgiven, we can have hope of heaven as we now have His victory and heaven is ours now and forever.

As we go through our days with all sorts of little things going on, God is having us realizing the salvation of our souls. That's the biggest picture we can get.

What I Gave Up

After a move from a small quaint suburb to the big city and feeling claustrophobic among the tall buildings, I decided to take up hiking to lose some extra pounds and find nature on the weekends. All it took for me was one hike with a heavy backpack to make me think through what is essential for a walk up a mountain. About half way through the trip when I was getting tired and each step was becoming more of an effort, I did an inventory in my head about what I was carrying on my strained back.

For the next trip I weighed each item. I went looking for the lightest equipment, which I found those things made out of the lightest material is also the most expensive, but over miles on a hike, it is worth the cost, and I took out what I did not think I needed. I set my backpack on my bathroom scale, and it went down by a few pounds. The next hike went better, and with each hike I learn what were the very basic things needed for a walk in the woods.

Motivated by my hiking trips, I started to go through my closets and drawers. I became very deliberate about all that I had. This was my Walden's Pond where Henry David Thoreau spent two years looking at what was needed in life. I decided to become a minimalist.

I dumped all kinds of books, knick-knacks, clothes, shoes, and dishes into my trunk. Thrift stores looked forward to my coming. I did away with the clutter, and I found it easier to clean the house. I had more space to move about, and I bought a few plants that I could nurture and watch grow.

Looking at my backpack and my house that now have all just the essentials to sustain me simply, I thought about my whole life. If there is a scale to measure how many unnecessary burdens I was carrying, I would be tipping it over.

I wondered about how many situations and circumstances a person goes through in a life time. Each of them has its way of leaving things behind. Every day is filled with things that we label good or bad, and happy or sad.

When I was going through my backpack and closets, I made myself ask questions, "Why do I need this thing?" "What could be its purpose?" For the things in my heart and mind, I asked the same kind of questions.

As every year has seasons of change, so do our lives. A few years ago I went through a bad season. I reacted to a very difficult time that seemed to trigger every sin of my life to jump on me. I have a tendency to be hard on myself. Somehow I got the idea that a person is to be perfect.

I had a load of guilt, shame, and anger on me. Guilt because I knew that I knew better. It seemed to me that I had caused a lot of hurt in others by what I said and did. Shame because as I looked back at some of things that I messed up, I was not proud of what I had done. Anger because my life at many points did not turn out as I had hoped. I had many disappointments.

With guilt, shame, and anger in my heart and mind, I threw some of the best pity-parties. I asked, "Why me?" I thought that I was the only one who had difficulties in life. I became over-indulgent in things to try to ease the pain. The consequences of finding pleasure in unhealthy ways started to pile up. I was self-sabotaging my life. Nothing is worse than feeling sorry for oneself.

I was in a pit, and I had to get out of it. In one way, going down deep into the ugly stuff was a good thing. I met face to face all of my demons. If left unmet, they would still try to control me. I had to be painfully honest and admit that I was capable of thoughts and actions that did not reflect well of me.

But the journey of a broken life does not end in the pit. The beauty of being a child of a loving God is that we can come to Him and confess each sin. In the end, all I had to do was to sincerely say, "Lord, forgive me for I am a sinner."

After emptying my life of all my sins with repentance, I am now filled with only one necessary thing in me. Throughout my heart, I have a faith that says, "I'm a beloved child of God." With only having one status in a world of many things that can bring on confusion to the point of chaos, I need to keep my life going in only one direction. This one direction is going always to God as His child.

My apartment got down to a bed, some crates that I stacked a few things on, and a camping chair. For me, I needed to get down to the bones of what a person needs to have. Since that time I have added a couch and a desk, and my goal is to add things to make life comfortable yet uncomplicated. This all has made a good new beginning.

My apartment is on a busy street with sirens and loud music throughout the day and night, but it works well as my small cabin on a pond. To have peace, I tend to a faith that holds all essential things for me. I dump all that is heavy and unnecessary, so I can have empty places that can be filled with the good things of God's grace, which is most needed. I am sure if I got on a scale that weighed emotions and thoughts, I am now much lighter.

Living Indestructible

I've been a heavy meat-eater most of my life. Vegetables have never been a favorite. The way I figure is that cows eat grass, and I eat the cow in the way of a big hamburger or medium-rare steak. I get my greens that way.

But realizing that I'm not getting any younger and to flush out some arteries, I better change my diet. The surefire way to go is going more to farmer's markets and not so much to the butcher.

Convinced that getting more vegetables was the answer, but still not liking the idea of sitting down to a whole plate of them, I've heard about juicing. What I do is get together all of my vegetables and fruits like kale, celery, beets, apples, lemons, and all kinds of berries. I experiment with different variations. My favorite comes out a putrid shade of green that I call "Green Goodness." It looks awful but tastes great, and I think it is the best thing I have put inside of me for years.

After I eat "Green Goodness," I feel indestructible. I have new energy, and I am thinking I can do about anything. Superman better watch out as the number one superhero.

Although I am feeling indestructible, the reality is that bullets don't bounce off of me. Any of the superheroes don't have to be concerned about me taking over their jobs.

One of my jogging routes is around a cemetery. The path is exactly one mile. But no matter how many times I jog around that cemetery I will one day die and have my name on a headstone with my body under it.

Life is Good Today

By our very nature, humans are susceptible to all kinds of things. Even in the best of health, we can get sick. One little sting from a spider or a disease carrying mosquito, and we can get really ill. It doesn't take much to hurt us.

Stop and think for a moment about how you are at this moment. Do you have a place where you are hurting right now?

For a moment take an inventory of yourself from your toes to your head, and from your feelings to your mind. Maybe you have a sore toe from when you stubbed it when you got up in the middle of the night to go to the bathroom. Or you have chronic pain like arthritis in your hands that make it hard to open a jar of peanut butter. For me, my knees are sore, and I can really feel them when I go upstairs.

Are you dealing with a situation that has left you disappointed? Our reactions are red flags that tell us something is wrong. When we have anger, frustration, anxiety, or fear, these emotions are telling us that we have to take care of what is upsetting us. Our minds during this time can get clouded as we are upset and that makes for poor decision making and situations can only get worse.

The important thing to remember as we go through all of life's situations from the small irritating things to the horrific and tragic, that we can get hurt, but we are never harmed.

Getting hurt is like going to the dentist. When we have a cavity, the dentist needs to stick us with a shot of novacane that numbs us, so he can drill and fix the tooth. If he doesn't make it better, we may get a bad infection in the tooth that can go deep and can cause real bad pain.

If you remember with Job, God and Satan had a conference up in heaven about the boundaries that Satan could have as he was to inflict Job with hardships to test Job's faith. But God gave instructions to Satan that he could not harm Job.

Harm is when a person is knocked down so low that he or she can't get back up again. Satan gave Job a real big wallop. Job got close to giving up, but he did get back up after all that happened to him.

When we live by faith, we are indestructible. Nothing can harm us. Faith tells us how Jesus is the great destroyer of all harmful things. By Jesus' death and resurrection, he wiped out eternal death and the power of Satan over us. We are human and will sin, but we do have the Jesus' power over temptation, and if we do sin, we have by God's grace in Christ, forgiveness of every sin.

In anything that we face in this life, we can have hope and strength. By faith there is nothing that we can't do. To be real here, it does seem at times when some of life's really tough situations happen like a "last thing we want to hear" diagnosis from a doctor or waking up to the smell of smoke and standing outside as we watch our house burn to the ground and all we have is lost that we will never get back up again. But the word to watch here is "seem."

Things may seem bad at the time, but by faith we are indestructible. What would happen right now if you went back to your inventory of the things that are hurting you and you thought that these things may hurt you but can never harm you?

As much as I would like to have muscles like iron and be able to leap tall buildings, I am not a superhero. But I am a child of God, and I have His love and power in me, and by faith in all of what God has for me, I am indestructible and can face anything that comes my way.

Living Out Promises

While growing up and when I wanted something, I would ask my mom for it, and for most of the time her answer was, "We'll see." Like when we were at the grocery store, and it came to checking out, I would ask, "Mom, can I have a pack of gum?" She would say, "We'll see. I am not sure if I have that kind of money." I grew up thinking that there was special money for buying gum that was not part of the green paper money that I was always seeing. For gum, candy, and toys, there was a different kind of money that my mom needed to get those things.

With four kids and a tight budget, my mom and dad were sure to be real with us. They never made promises to us about stuff that we wanted. If they knew they were able to get things for us, they said, "Yes." We hardly ever heard "No." But they did say many times, "We'll see."

I grew up understanding that our mom and dad wanted to give us things. When they said, "We'll see," it meant that they were trying to put a plan together to get that something that we wanted. One year my brother, my sister, and I wanted new bikes. My youngest sister was into dolls, so she wanted a house for them.

Every time we went to the store, I wandered back to the bike section, and I then I took my little sister to the toy department for her to look at dollhouses. My brother, sisters, and I decided to put the bikes and the dollhouse on our Christmas lists, which we made up in September. You guessed it. When my mom and dad looked at the lists, they said together, "We'll see." That Christmas there were three bikes and a dollhouse in the living room.

We were hardly ever disappointed about things. Our mom and dad kept their word to us. Their "No" meant certainly there was no way it was going to happen, and they followed through when they said, "Yes." And when they said, "We'll see," we knew they would try their best for us, and we knew we had to be patient and wait.

For kids to grow up healthy, moms and dads need to live out their promises. When parents model how they follow up on their commitments, their children learn about trust, which helps them now and later in life as they connect with others.

Promises make the world go around. They are the key to strong whole relationships. When promises are kept, life goes well as words turn into actions. When promises are broken, things get stalled with a lot of heavy talk and little action on all of those words.

For any of us, the best thing to do when making a promise is to be real about it. If there is something that comes up that needs a commitment, but if we know we may not follow through with it, the best thing to do is not to make that promise in the first place.

Boundaries are good to make and keep. I am one those persons who has to satisfy his ego by saying "Yes" to everything. Actually it is okay to say "No" to those things that I do not think that I can do or are not good for the other person. It has taken a lot of trial and error to find out that "No" is the best answer for many circumstances with some people, even when they are in difficult situations. I am learning that problems always work out somehow. I don't have to solve everything.

God gives us the perfect example of making and keeping promises. Right after Adam's fall into sin, God made a promise that He would send a Savior into the world. All through the Old Testament everything pointed to that promise. Every sacrifice of an animal was a type of sacrifice that showed how this Savior would come and give his own life up by giving his own body and blood for the forgiveness of sins once and for all. This all did happen when God's own Son, Jesus, was born into this world and was the living out of this promise when he lived, died, and rose for us to give us eternal life.

With all the promises that God made to people from His promise to take care of the Israelites in the wilderness to His promise when St. Paul had an affliction in his body and wanted it taken away. God told Paul that

His grace is sufficient for him. In the same way, we can believe that God by His grace is taking care of us in every way.

What we need to do to really know God's promises is to be sure that when we make a promise that we are sure to live it out. It is like the petition in the Lord's Prayer where we ask God to forgive us as we have forgiven others. We will not know God's forgiveness and what it all does for us if we do not forgive others.

If we do not keep our promises, then we will not know how God keeps his promises to us. When we are living out our promises, we are showing how we know that God lives out His promises in Christ.

When my son was growing up, we liked to fish and golf. If I said we were going on Saturday to the golf course or lake, I tried by best to make it. As a pastor and on call, sometimes things came up, but I always tried to make sure those times were very few, and if I could not make it then, I would make it up to him very quickly.

When we live out our promises, we are showing Jesus-who is God's living promise in us.

Squared-Up and Strong

My grandfather made furniture-some real cool things like dressers with secret drawers. My dad was the best handyman and could fix anything from a toaster that didn't pop up toast any longer to our old engine in our big old station wagon. My uncles were cracker-jack carpenters and built our garage in a day. My older brother can design and build anything. In high school shop, I was lucky to make a shoebox.

I guess we all have our talents, but you would think a little bit of carpentry skills would rub off on me-makes sense if I got some skills-doesn't it? I keep pounding, but all I get are crooked nails.

I have been a teacher for many years, and it's a fine profession. Teaching works for me, but at times I am envious of carpenters as they build something. Teachers and carpenters have things in common like making plans and doing the steps to make those plans work. But teachers are never sure quite what their work with a student has accomplished. Sure, there are test scores to see if a student is learning what is being taught, but life goes on, and after the student leaves my classroom, I often wonder what the student has done with his or her life. Some students have come back and shared their successes, but I wonder about some who struggled and had troubles.

The carpenter can stand back and look at the house he has just built and say, "Job, well done!" and move on to another building project. The house has been inspected and proved to hold to code. The house is squared-up and strong. From foundation to roof and chimney the house will shelter people from storms and cold. The house will be a home to a family where they will live and make memories.

Life is never quite down-is it? We are all kind of a work in progress, even for the carpenter's life. No matter what we do for a living we are all works in progress. The best life is the one that is squared-up and strong like a well-built house.

For instance, as I look at my students and myself as teacher, I am thinking I am learning just about as much stuff about life as they are. Teaching is a noble and also tough profession as it requires a lot of patience, understanding, and perseverance in today's culture that does not often value the effort and work needed to learn.

So I need to keep building myself up in all of my inner parts to try to keep doing well. By inner parts, I am not talking about my spleen or anything. I am talking about the mysterious place where we have our courage, hopes, and values. You know those things that we believe in that motivates us and gets us going in the toughest of times.

If I am not thinking and doing the things I need to build up, I can easily get discouraged as I see a world that is often chaotic and seems to be losing its moral compass.

From the time after the fall into sin to the time of Noah when people had lost the direction of God's good will, God thought that the only answer was to drown them in a flood and start over with the one righteous man who was left. God had Noah build an ark, their new home during the flood.

In the ark, God promised Noah and his family would be safe. The ark was built with very precise specifications. God knew what He was doing when he gave Noah the instructions for the building of the ark. The ark had to hold lot of animals and keep Noah's family safe as the ark tossed about during the torrential rains that would flood the earth for a long period of time.

The rains came and went. The earth was dry again, and the ark landed. Noah, his family, and the animals were safe and left the ark to start a new beginning.

In much the same way, God gave Solomon very specific instructions to build the first permanent temple. Up until now the people worshiped God in tents, but now they were to have a solid building of wood and stone.

Solomon built the temple to God's design. Now, the nation of Israel could worship God here, but they also knew all that God had for them was here. In this temple, they knew that they would always find God's peace.

God gives us today His way to build our houses. You got it figured out. I'm not talking about the houses we call our homes, though those are important, too. I'm talking about our spiritual houses where all those inner parts are. We need to build up our beliefs because this old sinful world and our own sinful fleshes try to destroy the house-it's all kind of like the big old wolf who liked to huff and puff and blow things down.

First, we have to make sure our foundation is built on the Gospel. Believing what Jesus has done for us when he went to the cross to die for our sins is that foundation. From the overflowing of forgiveness of every sin and the gift of eternal life, we can move on to build our house that will hold all of the good things that God has for us.

This house is perfectly squared-up and strong because it is built by God and the foundation is His, Son, Jesus who dwells in us giving us courage, hope, and values. When we go through life with all of the stormy situations that can come up, we go to the house where there is always complete comfort and peace.

That Light Bulb Thing

After the application that had a few long essay questions, I got a letter saying I was scheduled for my final interview for my entrance into seminary. On that day I walked into a conference room with the president of the seminary and several professors at the table. I was invited to sit down, and I was looking at the faces of some of the world's renowned theological scholars. To say I was as nervous as a guy in ancient Rome thrown in with the lions.

It turned out that many of the questions were from the application. I thought I was doing well, and near the end of the interview, the seminary's president looked at me directly, and asked, "Why do you want to become a pastor?" That question was one of the essay questions, but my mind went blank. I paused for a second and blurted out, "It's that light bulb thing."

I saw the confused faces, and quickly continued blurting out the answer. I told them about teaching music and about one of my trumpet students, Jason, who was in a solo competition. The piece had a few challenging parts with a high note that Jason had difficulty hitting. We worked on it and tried several ways to get to the note. It had been a struggle, but he was getting it about a week before the competition. On the day of the competition, when it came to the high note, I closed my eyes, and Jason did awesome. The note came out in a beautiful tone. After the piece, Jason smiled, and so did I. I saw a light in Jason's eyes-that moment when things connect is the light bulb thing that teachers live for.

I went on to tell the president that I want to help people see the Gospel. My nerves were all gone now as I told him that connection to the love of

Christ is the light bulb thing that I think I can do as a pastor. The president looked at me and said, "Good answer. Welcome to seminary."

I've been a pastor for over twenty years now, and I've added many stories of light bulbs when people were comforted by the Gospel. In some ways, I've felt like Thomas Edison when he was working on getting a light bulb that would last beyond a few seconds. It took over two-hundred experiments to get the light bulb to stay lite to bring light to people's homes. When Edison was asked about the failed experiments, he said, "I found two hundred ways on how to not make a light bulb."

Teaching and sharing the light of Christ to a world that is dark with sin at times takes many tries. We live in a world with a culture that in many ways is opposed to the light that is in God's Word.

I saw a documentary that chronicled Billy Graham's ministry. Billy Graham said a preacher should carry a bible around one arm and a newspaper around the other. His sermons throughout the years had a pattern. He began with talking about the news of the day. In the sixties he talked about the war in Viet Nam and the riots of the Civil Rights movement. Through the decades of his ministry, Billy Graham used current events of other conflicts to show that the world is in dark sin and needs the light of Christ.

Today we still have a world that is dark in sin and needs the light of Christ. Our culture has almost died with little life in it that is close to the will of God. The newspaper today continues to report of conflict like terrorists' bombings, refuges are all over the world as governments clash, and riots rage as tensions continue between races.

Billy Graham would still have material for his sermons as far as we need a Savior from sin. Since the fall into sin, humans have always needed to be saved. From the wickedness of Noah's day to David's sin of adultery and from disobedience of the nation of Israel to the sin of Paul when he persecuted Christians, we have always needed an intervention between us and the punishment of eternal death for our sins.

Maybe the light bulb switched on in many people's minds when the flood waters started to reach their noses. David did get a light bulb go on when he was confronted with his sin. The Israelites saw the light of God's grace when they did repent, and St. Paul did have a light bulb experience when Jesus spoke to him on the road to Damascus.

The Gospel according to St. John opens with telling how Jesus has come to be the light of all people. In Jesus' light we see God's grace and love, which gives us forgiveness of every sin and eternal life. Now we can go and be a light to others, so they can have what we have in Christ.

At first we may want to avoid the culture knowing it is sinful. But avoiding it will only separate us from it. We might also want to fly above the culture, so we do not look like we condone anything in the culture, but again this will separate us from it. We are not engaged with the culture, but we enter with the light of Christ. For the sin that is in the darkness, Jesus will see, judge, and condemn, and he will also give an opportunity for whoever is sinful to come to him in repentance.

The darkness of our culture can change to light. We are going into the enemy's territory, but we go equipped with a powerful light that can transform a messed up and chaotic culture. God wants all things to come to Him and know His good will and His great love and care. It's all about that light bulb thing that disciples of Christ live for.

Hear Jesus Asking, "How Can I Help You, Today?"

Good service is the key to any good business. Walking into a restaurant, the first thing a hungry customer wants to hear is, "What can I get for you, today?" As my stomach gurgles and churns, I always like it when the waitress is pleasant and attentive. My hunger pains subside a little just knowing I am being cared for.

When we are with a friend and talking about life, near the end of our sharing, we might ask each other, "What can I do for you, today?" It is always good to hear that I am being offered help. The big comfort is their concern to listen to me. Now there is a technique to use if a friend is not around. It is called, "Rubber duck debugging." This is where you talk out loud to a rubber duck. Of course a friend is better, but at least with a duck you can hear your own thoughts.

The point is that we can never under estimate the power there is when we open up and share our lives. In our sharing, we hear ourselves, and often it seems as the words leave our mouths and hit our own ears, we find the solutions to our problems. Love is circular, and in this love, we help each other out, even if it is just by listening to each other. And friends have often come back when the intent was on helping me and said, "You know, Tom, our talk helped me out, too."

I think when it really comes down to it, we need to solve our own problems; we have to make a conscious decision about a change in our thoughts about how we will think about a situation, but there is still something to the fact that we always need others for support. Our situations in life go better when we are there for each other. So as service is good for business, when we take on a servant role, it is good for relationships.

Jesus left his heavenly throne to come to earth to be a servant. Only in a servant role could Jesus accomplish his purpose to save people from the punishment of sin, eternal death. From the moment Jesus was born in a lowly estate in a stable to his death on the cross where he took the punishment for all people's sins, we see his humility and all that he wanted to do was to serve.

Although Jesus is a prophet, priest, and king, and as he is God the Son, and as he has all under his feet, Jesus still takes the role of servant. While he walked this earth, he healed, fed, and cared for people in their situations. Jesus identified himself with the weak and those on the outskirts of society.

All that Jesus wanted to do was to help people where they were at. Jesus wanted people to hear him asking, "What can I do for you, today?" He knew people were in need, and he knew he had all to help anyone in any circumstance. He spent the whole day with Zacchaeus. With the woman at the well, he gave her all the time she needed, and even when Jesus was dying, he was there to help the thief on the cross next to him.

Can you hear Jesus asking you, "What can I do for you for you, today?" In our situations that often are stressful and cause us to have emotions like anger, anxiety, frustration, and guilt, we know something is wrong, but we do not know how to let go of the suffering that we have. So we hold on to these emotions and our situations do not get any better as we are stuck in our bad feelings and the drama of those feelings, and nothing ever gets better when our thoughts and feelings are negative.

The one good purpose of sadness is that it alerts us that something needs to be done, and what is to be done is to hear Jesus asking, "What can I do for you?" This question comes out of great love and care. And we know this love is real because by we already know what Jesus' love has done for us.

Faith tells us that Jesus has already loved us so much that he went to the cross to die for our sins and to beat sin, death, and Satan by rising from the dead. If Jesus has given his life for us to battle our enemies that can hurt us for all of eternity, we can know he is here today to help us with every need.

Too often we see God as an angry God who is looking to punish us because of our sins. It could be said that God is angry over our sins because God is a just God and does not like sin. But he poured out all of his anger on his own Son, so we do not have to take that punishment. God now out of his grace and mercy is pleased with us and gives his Son, Jesus, to help us in every way.

To be sure, we are to help one another and see ourselves as servants to each other, but when it comes to problems, we really need to work it out by ourselves. It is like faith; no one can believe for us, we need to have our own faith. We can listen to each other and support each other, but we need to sink into solving the problems with all that we got. And we have a lot. On the one hand we need to get active and start thinking right and doing right, but the truth is we can't do anything without the help of Jesus, so at any time in any situation, we can hear Jesus asking, "What can I do for you, today?"

The Better Help

I was talking with my new neighbor, Fred. You know one of those conversations over the fence when you pause from doing chores in the yard. From previous over the fence conversations, I have told him that I am not into social media. I tried it, but keeping up with everything was soaking up a lot of time. Okay, you can call me old school, but I don't want to be glued to my phone all day.

I like FaceTime to connect with my son who is away at college, and I call and visit my mom, and visit as often as I can an uncle who lives in an assisted living place. I try to keep up with my brother and sisters by sending pictures when I am doing something different and exciting. With one friend, Joe, I call often and text at least once a day, "How's it going?"

When Fred sees me, he keeps trying to get connect with me in cyber world. He says he has over three hundred friends and counting on Facebook and follows many others. I am just wondering what time he has to get up in the morning and go to bed at night to have real relationships with all of these people.

I have heard it said that if a person has one or two good friends in a lifetime, he is doing well. To me, a friend cares for me warts and all, and I am there for him whenever he needs me.

When Joe and I ask every day, "How's it going?" We actually mean it to its very core. I don't know about you, but most of my days are pretty much the same old stuff. But some days can get rough. When those kind of days come, we make an extra point to meet for coffee.

Joe and I have this thing that we call the "five minute dumping rule." For five minutes each, we get to tell each other all that is going on in our lives. If we go longer than five minutes, we would be just repeating ourselves and start going into self-pity and blaming the world for our problems, which can get nauseating.

We listen and talk. We ask each other questions that help us to go into a new direction. The conversations are deep as we go into the heart of the matter that is often ugly at first. But we work through it all and help each other to get moving forward in a good direction.

I do not think I can do all of this sharing with hundreds of friends on Facebook. I have to say I am a little picky when it comes to sharing and from where I get my help from.

I guess it's only natural to reach out to anything for help when there is a problem. If I'm drowning, and someone throws be a little rubber ducky, I would grab it. But the best thing is a life-saver that has been certified.

I have been blessed with a good son, a caring family, and a good friend. We are great helps to each other. What we all have in common is that we get our help from the Lord, and when we help each other, what we are doing is sharing what God has given us.

God has given us the better help in His Son, Jesus. With Jesus we can do all things through him. That is his promise to us.

Think of it like a bowl. A bowl is only useful when it is empty. Right?

The better thing we can do is to fill up our empty bowls with the promises of God. Imagine in our bowls that all we have are all the things that Jesus has done for us. We have bowls filled with forgiveness of every sin. And they are overflowing with love, strength, and hope for every situation that comes up in our often complicated lives. We live in a messy world, but with our bowls of faith, we can get through anything.

The most important thing here about faith is that we start with empty bowls. Often our bowls are filled with all kinds of things. In our bowls we have anxieties and fears, and we like to put in our own ideas about how life should go.

So between all of the worries of life and our own egos of trying to work out our lives contrary to God's will for our lives, there is no room for the things we need from God to have good faiths.

In our church we confess our sins in a general way where we say for the most part, "We have sinned in thought, word, and deed, and have not lived our lives according to the will of God." This confession is an emptying of our bowls, so we can hear God's forgiveness and get them filled with His grace.

Now with the promises of God in our bowls, we are good to go to enter our lives again. As we go through the minutes and hours of our days, we need support. All kinds of circumstances come our way that want to get back in our bowls and push out the promises of God. Life can be tough and scary, and our egos think they have the better way. But Jesus is always the better help.

I am blessed to have people around me with great bowls of faith that are overflowing with God's promises. If any of our bowls are running low or are getting mixed in with worries and selfish kind of stuff, we help each to get them filled up again with God's word.

I am thinking I should be doing more with social media since it's the way our world is going, but I will always be sure to get the better help for me, who is always Jesus.

Standing in Heaven's Line

Sometimes I hear that people think that they are so certain about something, but it all turns out wrong. "I was so sure that I picked the right numbers for the lottery this week. How could I have lost?" "I thought I could be a casual drug user like my friend told me. I didn't think I could become addicted." "It was all a small affair. Really, I did not mean for my marriage to fall apart." "My temper has been cool lately, but I still get stressed, so what can it hurt when I do lash out at times." "With her smug attitude, a little gossip that gets back to her won't hurt her."

I know I can get that way. At times, I think just a little sin here and there can really do no wrong. As I go about my life, I see other people do worse things. For the most part, I am a pretty good person. No one is perfect. A faultless and flawless life is just too much to ask of anyone.

The truth is that in my mind, I can justify about anything, and I can be so certain that just a little wrong is not really all that bad. The battle to do what is absolutely right goes on in my head every day. I know right from wrong, but I have to fight to make good decisions.

For as much as the whole purpose of our faith is to get to heaven, we really do not know too much about it. Jesus talks about mansions that he is preparing in heaven for us; the apostle John talks about a city of jewels and gold; we know we will see our Lord fact to face one day, and that's enough information to want to there.

But getting to heaven has some concern for me. Jesus gives a picture what the entrance to heaven looks like, and from this picture it does not seem that entering heaven is an easy task.

The entrance to heaven is by a narrow door, which means it is not a door for everyone. Only people who have known Jesus in this life on earth will get into heaven. To know Jesus is just not to know who he is as the Son of God, for the devil and evil people know that about him, but they do not have a relationship with him. They are not connected to him by a faith that believes that Christ is their Savior from sin, death, and Satan.

But it is not enough just to know Jesus as a Savior. Faith that is in the heart also has to be seen in the acts we do is our lives, and that gets to be a concern for me at times. As I said, I have my struggles to always do good things.

My picture of heaven is seeing all the saints, including my loved ones who have died in the faith, praising Jesus who sits on a throne. It is a glorious sight, but first there is the entrance where there are many people. Outside the gates of heaven are people who are wanting to get in, but they are finding that they are not going to be able to get through the gate. They are yelling out Jesus' name, but he is saying, "I don't know you."

This is all after they have died. In their lives, they knew of Jesus, but they did not have a relationship with him, and now it is too late. It is like a line in the song "O When the Saints Go Marching In." I really do want to be in that number that can get through the door to heaven with all of the other saints, but I do know that I am not always connected to Jesus in my life. I know I fall way short of doing God's will.

Lines are difficult things. I don't know anyone who really likes to be in a line. I always seem to get in the line where the person in front of me needs a price check, and the guy to do it is on break.

So one day I am standing in heaven's line, and the line is long. I look ahead and see some people being turned away. This makes me nervous now because I am thinking if they are getting turned away, I might get turned away, too. I know that I am a poor miserable sinner. In my sin, I am disconnected from Jesus.

I see another person get turned away, and he looked like a good guy. Right now, I know I don't have a chance and begin to walk away, but then I feel a touch on my shoulder. It is Jesus, and he says, "Where are you going, Tom?"

Surprised, I turn around, and I about to explain that I have seen the door of heaven and that there is no way that I can get through such a narrow door with my baggage of sin. Jesus nods his head, but he opens the door for me, Like Saint Paul, I look at my life and see that I am wretched person, but then I realize I am saved by grace and praise God for that gift. By faith I am connected to Jesus now and for all of eternity. I will make it through heaven's line to the front door.

As long as I am in this sinful flesh, life is a struggle. What I need to do is to acknowledge that fact, but also know that the same grace that connects me to Jesus at heaven's door is the same grace that makes us in a close relationship now, for Jesus is not only the door opener, he is the door that I need to enter every day to have strength for life's struggles.

A Good Failure

To her team just before the big game in the locker room, the coach says, "Failure is not an option," We don't want to fail. When it comes down to success or failure, we want to do well, especially when we have put all of our effort into something.

We have our expectations on how we want circumstances to turn out for us. When we are happy with the results of what we have done, we feel successful, but when things do not turn out well, we consider that we have failed.

Failure is not an option that we want to make, but failures do happen and maybe happen even more often than our successes. Is it possible that we should not be so quick to shed our failures but to find some use for them?

We learn more from our failings than anything else in our lives. Failure is the best teacher. With failure, we ask, "What all went wrong?" And in the answers to that question, we can move forward in our discoveries.

Inventors can count on failure. The Wright brothers did not soar for hours the first time they flew their plane. Abraham Lincoln lost a few elections before he became one of this country's best presidents. To get a man on the moon it took many explosions at the launch pad, but now spaceflight is a fact.

We need to make a few if not many failed attempts at whatever we are doing. We don't often get it right the first time. I think the people who have moved on to great things were not afraid to fail at the beginning. They realized their failures but did not let them pile up in the negative column. They looked at them to learn from them and then moved forward. We do not discard our losses, but we keep them to give them purpose and meaning.

In my life when it was not going well at all, and it seemed like life was one bad thing after another, the more that I tried to fix my life, the more that it got more messed up. And when I looked at my life, it is not that my attempts were failures, but I thought that I was a failure.

Failure can be inspirational. I can just hear Saint Paul say, "What a wretched man I am." Here is Paul who is one person that can be said is doing his best to do God's will, but he still finds himself failing in many ways. Paul knows that he is a sinner. Any person on any day in some way fails to do God's will.

In one sense, sin never turns out well. Sin always hurts others and ourselves. But this is not to say that sin is the end. Sin never has the final word. Things can work out even after we have had a mountain of sin fall on us. God loves us enough to keep after us, so we can see that we need to turn to Him. With God nothing is ever lost. All comes together to His glory.

When I was a kid and broke a toy, for a while I would hide the toy. I did not want to get my mom and dad angry because I did not take care of my stuff. To play again with my toys, I had to admit what I had done, so all I could do was to go to my mom and dad and say, "I'm sorry. Can you fix it?"

Moving forward in life, we want to be rid of all of our failings. On our shelves, we display our trophies and ribbons-we don't put out our bad attempts for others to see.

Humans have stained the earth with sin from the beginning of time. Adam tried to hide from God after his sin, but where can we hide from God who has made all of heaven and earth?

The most important thing about sin is simply to admit that we have done wrong. God wants us to come to Him with our broken and sorrowful spirits. Admitting that we have fallen way short of God's will and glory is a good thing.

Now, we can begin to turn things around and start moving in a new direction.

Life can shift from the dark to the light. What we need to remember that this movement from darkness to the light is natural. Every day has a cycle of night and going to day and back to night. And we have to remember that God created darkness to fill the void. The night has a purpose. It separates us from the light and gives us a contrast. In the night, God is still moving and working.

So in our failures that seem dim and without purpose, God is working and doing what He thinks is best for us. God's gifts are always better than our plans.

I am not sure that I would ever wake up and say this is a good day to fail. It is possible to get lost in optimism. Sometimes our dreams can get too big, and we miss what is real. Reality is that the day will probably have some mistakes and even big mess ups. Failure keeps us grounded in what is real. In one way I think I just need to get better at failing and that keeps me humble. In another way I should be working towards success and that keeps me hopeful.

A day will have sin of many kinds as we are reminded we are only human, and as humans we need forgiveness. The beauty of any day is that we can rejoice and praise God that it is a day of forgiveness and salvation. With this in mind, any day, even with failures, can be good.

The Person of Romans Seven

I've been saying "stupid" a lot lately. It's a word that I've never liked, but at just about every little turn of frustration, I say, "That's stupid." Last winter was rough and has left potholes about every five feet, and when I dodge one crater, I hit another. With every thud, I say, "We can send a man to the moon, but we can't make asphalt to last one winter. That's stupid."

A friend, Larry, and I get together for coffee every week to talk about stuff in our lives. We have this thing called, "The two minute dumping rule." It used to be five minutes, but we had found that after three minutes the dumping got to be a little nauseating as we crossed the line into self-pity. So for a strict two minutes we tell each other our problems without interruption saying whatever comes to our minds.

I was telling Larry about how in a situation with a co-worker I let my ego get the better of me, and it only caused further conflict. Larry looked at me when I got done with my two minutes and said, "Tom, sin makes us stupid."

Larry did not have to be so blunt, but he is right. Sin does make us stupid. For me the definition of "stupid" is that we know better about doing something that is bad for us, but we do it anyway.

I have been in a high self-reflective mood lately. For most of life I have always been a contemplative type of person who is always asking questions about myself and the world around me. The questions led to answers that led to more questions. So now at fifty-five, I thought I would ask some tough questions about my life. At my age, I'm thinking I should have some deep thoughts about a meaningful life that will lead to actions for the benefit of others.

The conflict at work and some other things in my life seemed to be telling me that I should be further along in my life. Logic and emotion needed to get more in balance.

When I was younger I was always anxious about my future, and now I am living that future and am okay. What is strange is that I am still am stressed about the years ahead. I would think I would have learned by now that worrying about tomorrow does not get me anywhere.

The reason I think that word "stupid" has been on mind and a little on my lips is that the more that I get this picture of my future-self the more that I realize how stupid I have been about many things. I really did not know how bad I was until I tried to do better.

In my devotion time, I read a prayer by Alfred Lord Tennyson, "Oh that the man would arise in me that the man I am may cease to me." Then I read this by D.L. Moody, "I have more trouble with D.L. Moody than with any person I know." When I read these things, I got to thinking that I need to quit the nonsense in my life and move to a new me.

Words came back to me from Scripture that have always made me think because they are about struggling with what seems an addiction. Surprisingly, St. Paul, the great apostle in Romans chapter seven, wrote them. If anyone has their act together, it has to be St Paul. He was the one to set the early church straight with sound doctrine about salvation in Christ, but he still struggled with sin in his life. In Romans Chapter Seven, he talks about his struggle with what seems a very bad habit.

St Paul says, "For I do not do the good that I want, but the evil I do not want is what I keep on doing." Paul knew better about something he was doing. He knew it was wrong, but he did it anyway. I wonder if he felt stupid like I do after I do something wrong although I had known better not to do it. The point is that every human being struggles with the things we do, and we all mess up at times.

This person in Romans Chapter Seven is every Christian. What we need to do is to get to know this person in this chapter. When we get to know this person, we will find who we are in God's love and grace. At times, we go in the wrong direction that we do not want to go in, but we go there anyways. This bad direction is a sin, and it is our sinful nature that makes us do it. Paul realizes that it is the sin that lives in him, and he can't do anything about it. As long as we live and walk on this earth, we are plagued by sin.

But in a sudden turn of thought just as he thinks his own mind and body will do him in, he sees that Christ can rescue him from sin. He exclaims that he is now saved and gives thanks to Christ. Life is now good in Christ, and he can move forward in life in God's grace.

It is not that we are stupid, but we choose to do stupid things at times. The sin that is in us will try to make us do all kinds of things that we really do not want to do. But just as we are about to be done in by sin, we can see God's grace in Christ.

I have done well for the most part, but I also have thrown a lot of wrenches in God's handiwork. To get to be more of whom I am meant to be in Christ, the best I can do is to get to know the person of Romans Chapter Seven.

God's High Thoughts of You

A woman went to her pastor to seek some counsel about a difficult time that she was having. It seemed to her that a lot of problems were piling up in her life. While talking through the situation, the pastor asked questions to try to understand all that had been happening with her. After the woman said all that she could say with tears in her eyes, the pastor said, "That is a very heavy load that you are carrying. This all requires a lot of strength and courage. God must think very highly of you for to you have such burdens." The woman lifted her head up and said with a slight smile, "I wish God would not think so highly of me."

But that's the point. The pastor did get it right. God does think very highly of us. After all, we are His children, and God wants the best for us. I can see what the woman is saying, too. We would like to go around trials than through them.

God has made us to be forward moving people, but often we move forward through trials. We are to always be moving towards a Christ-like character, which is a tall order as Christ was perfect. But we can build up to have all of the attributes of Christ. We can have his goodness and strength. The way to get this character is through trials.

We have a faith of love and fear. This duality of our faith is something we can get easily with our minds, but in the day to day living of our lives where problems can seem to be piling up, how faith can get us through can get confusing.

What I mean that faith can get confusing is that at times we can't understand when life is heavy with troubles how God is working a good thing in us.

God loves us and forgives our many sins through Christ's death on the cross where he took the punishment for our sins. Yes, we only have this forgiveness by faith, and how Jesus us loved us so much that he willingly went to the cross to suffer and die for sinners is beyond our comprehension. But that is the depth of His love for us. And we by faith have new life in Him and have His strength for every day until we meet Him in heaven.

So what we have in Christ given to us by God the Father is an awesome love. By God the Father's grace we have everything. But then, we also have to understand that God is our judge. And as our judge, he is to be feared. Now, many times in Scripture we hear in places like at Jesus' birth with the angel's announcement to the shepherds that they are not to be afraid. After the first Easter, Jesus tells his disciples not to be afraid. But there are also many verses that tell us to fear God.

We are told not to be afraid, so that we know that God is very approachable. Our God is awesome and is all powerful, but He wants us to know that He is here to help us in every way. In the places where we are told to fear God, this fear is not a fear that trembles with a feeling that God will harm us. This fear is meant to be a fear that shows respect.

God is a judge that is to be feared, for He does not give a glancing look at sin. We are to have no doubt that God does not want us to sin. All it takes is one sin to mess us up, and with every sin, there are hard consequences. Sin always takes us away from God and His desire for us to live good lives.

At every point of our lives, we need to know that God has our best interests in mind. If it seems that God is coming down hard on us, it is only because He is disciplining us as a loving parent who cares for a child. God does not us to drift away from his care. And He is always developing us to be better people who are always going towards to being like the perfect model of His Son.

We are like a beautiful garden. God has given us a plot where there are the most luscious plants and flowers. They are green and full of reds and purples and yellows. But we come along and throw seeds of weeds into the garden and stones into the fertile soil. When we keep sinning and ruining what Christ has done for us by His pure life and death, we should be asking ourselves, "Why do I want to ruin the beauty that God has so graciously given to me?"

In our answer to that self-imposed question, we can answer by a faith that is both love and fear. By God's love shown to us in Christ, we know we are forgiven of every sin. And by fear, we know that God is very serious us for us to move forward without our old sins in the way to a new life.

Maybe we would like at times for God to leave us alone, and I think He does at times. I am not saying that we are ever out of His love, but He lets us go off in our own directions. I think He does this so we can see that it just doesn't work out that way at all. But He always brings us back, usually by some difficult time. God never want us to go back or stay stuck. He will keep us moving forward until we reach the goal our faith, our heavenly home. After all we are His beloved children brought to Him by His Son's precious blood, so God can't help but think very highly of us.

The Uncomfortable Life

As I'm looking more towards retirement, I am trying to look at the possibilities for my senior years that are quickly approaching. I put these options into three categories. The first one is to retire rich, but I think I missed that goal as soon as I got out of high school and choose a major that just didn't have any promise of making any real kind of money, but it has a been a very satisfying career. Then, I thought about that I would like to be comfortable in life with no financial worries, but my life has been for the most part getting by with just making it to pay the bills. I have just scratched along to make a budget work, and at times, I had just a little bit left over. So my last choice is that my retirement will be pretty much the same, and I am okay with that.

With a lot of talk about the economy these days, it seems that there are concerns that the any kind of financial security is slipping away, and we may be going to not be able to save much for a rainy day, if not even for just a morning with a few drizzles. Facing a tough economy and a bad job market can bring some anxiousness and worry. Those ends of income and expenses just do not seem like they want to meet at times.

In these days when I am counting my change to buy a gallon of milk, I try to remember what King David said about not being in want because the Lord is his Shepherd. For our everyday needs, the Lord will always provide as Jesus says that even God the Father makes sure the birds and flowers have all that they need, so it goes to figure that God will care for his beloved children.

As I look back at my life, I know that God has always provided for me, so I trust that he will provide for me all the way through my old age if I should make it that far. I am finding that as I get older that my goals are changing. My goal was to get more financially stable and get more money tucked away in different investments, which is not a bad goal. Money is a great tool that allows for many different things to happen, but my direction was to try to have a comfortable retirement. I dreamed of a log cabin by a lake and to catch up on a lot of fishing. I checked out that dream, it does not come cheap as the price of land is high. These days trees and quiet is prime real estate.

Going back to King David, he knew he was walking in the valley of the shadow of death. In his life as a king, he knew he had enemies. He walked in danger all the way, but he did not fear. As he had many challenges that might even cost him his life, he believed his Lord was with him every step of the way with His protection. With the Lord beside him, David faced the high demands and the challenges of being the ruler of God's people.

As Christians, we are to answer God's call to bring His love in Christ to a hurting world. Going out in this world may take us out of even more than financial security. We never really know what the Lord has planned for us. Sarah had a baby when she was way past childhood bearing age. Moses walked many years in the desert leading the nation of Israel to the Promised Land. Having some sort of physical problem, St. Paul took long missionary trips. The apostle John was banished to an island where he wrote Revelations. We never know how a life is going to turn out and what God will have us doing.

But we do know that whatever God does have us doing it is his good and holy desire for us just as it was with his Son, Jesus. It was God's will for Jesus to come down from heaven to earth to be born in a lowly stable. Jesus lived a simple life in a carpenter's family in a small town. During his ministry, he didn't have a home as he went from town to town to teach about the kingdom of God. And all of this time, he knew he was going to the cross to take the punishment for the sins of the world.

Going to the cross was on Jesus' mind throughout his ministry, he knew he had to do his Father's will, but he also knew how demanding it was going to be. On the night before his death, he prayed for the cup of suffering to be taken away if it could, but he accepted that it was his destiny to go to the cross.

As I think about moving forward in my life and knowing that God will always take care of me, I am coming to see more and more that as hard as I worked to get comfortable, something always comes along to take me out of my comfort zone. I thought challenges were for just meant for the young at heart, but as I was at one time twenty-one and had to learn what it meant to be that age and every age after that, I have to learn now what it means to be fifty-five and hopefully fifty-six and many years after that.

Challenges keep happening at any age, even for those who are older and supposedly wiser. God wants to use us for his purposes and sometimes those things are difficult. If I get uncomfortable with a new circumstance, I will try to remember what we sing at Easter, "I am content, My Savior Lives." At all times at any age, my soul is at peace.

About the Author

Dr. Thomas E Engel, a pastor for over twenty five years, grew up in Des Plaines, a suburb of Chicago. After high school, he taught piano and continued to teach piano while going to Middle Tennessee State University. Finishing with a major in English, he went to Concordia Seminary in St Louis where he received a Masters in Divinity. As an ordained pastor, he has served congregations in Minnesota, Kentucky, and Indiana while teaching college writing as an adjunct instructor. Now, he is serving as senior pastor at St Paul in Chicago. Also, he writes case studies and blogs for the Lutheran Church Missouri Synod's urban website and writes devotions for various Christian publications. In 2013, he earned a Doctor of Ministry in Pastoral Counseling.